"Sliding the blade further, he found it fitted exactly"

SHERLOCK
BY THE
SEA

Spike
Brown

Illustrated by

Karl Whiteley

Tower Bridge Books

Copyright © Spike Brown 2024

Illustrations © Karl Whiteley 2024

Spike Brown has asserted his right under the copyright, designs and patents act of 1988 to be identified as the author of this book.

All rights reserved.

No part of this publication may be reproduced, stored in a retrieval system, or transmitted in any form or by any means, electronic, mechanical, photocopying, recording or otherwise, without the prior permission of the copyright owner.

A catalogue record of this book is available from the British Library

Contents

The Marrow Grower	1
The Mews Mystery	17
A Surfeit of Ice Cream	36
Train to West Grinstead	49
The Bird Table Thief	70
Fumes of Saphir Médaille d'Or	82
Platform Vandal	110
Pebblesea Lighthouse	123
Mr. Falcon Smith	140
The Lost Pudding	155
Sally Sudbury's Christmas Tree	173
The Worth Valley Mystery	189
The Old Man of the Sea	210
The Bluebell Special	225
The Pebblesea Murders	251

For Siobhan & Sandra

The Marrow Grower

"Good morning Mr. Winstanley, I trust your marrows prosper?" enquired elderly Mr Holmes, putting down his shopping basket. The day was boiling hot, sunny, and sparkling. Removing his deerstalker hat, he wiped his brow with a hanky. Stood outside the City & Counties Bank along the High Street, the venerable old Sussex village of Findon nestled betwixt coast and the southern downs, the other gentleman raised his tweed cap offering Holmes a charming smile.

Mr Winstanley had retired and retreated to the country after working in the city as an accountant. He lived in one of the delightfully situated clergy houses, a much sought-after property close to the ancient church.

"Good morning Holmes, Mr Hampden assures me I have a fine chance of winning on Saturday," said he, unable to conceal a childish boastfulness. "How's your beekeeping?"

"Beekeeping," Holmes retorted. "Lord, that's long gone. I'm interested in golf these days, but I'm perfectly sure your vegetable marrow shall excel on all counts and prove to be supreme champion."

There was an audible clatter of metal striking stone.

"Hello, you've dropped something." Holmes knelt forward, wavering slightly, when he realised what lay on the sun-drenched pavement. He was surprised to see a silver engraved, small calibre pistol.

"Ha, ha, a mere toy that fires caps," joked the retiree, somewhat unconvincingly, hastily securing the pistol in his inner pocket. "Holmes, forgive my forwardness," said he in continuance, "you are, I know, no stranger to mysteries. I have, myself, a certain pressing matter that distracts me from my endeavours to grow marrows. I must, I *must*, I say, have clear analysis."

"If I can help in any way, I shall," answered Holmes. "Mr Winstanley, I trust this matter is in no way dangerous. Your armament, I refer to."

"Do not, I implore you, be alarmed, sir. My dear Holmes, the pistol is, I assure you, a mere replica. Perfectly harmless. Might we adjourn to the tea rooms," he proposed, "for China tea and scones?"

"Certainly," said Holmes, allowing Mr Winstanley to carry one of his wicker baskets.

The gentleman added, almost wistfully, "How's old Watson keeping? Not passed on, I trust. We none of us get any younger – must be in his late seventies by now."

"Coming up from Horsham to play on the links next weekend. Watson and I are golfing partners, and rather good at it."

The popular tea rooms were, as normal, crowded with old cats like Miss Briars and Miss Crighton-Lewis. Gossipy spinster ladies who, it must be said, appeared to shower appreciative glances in the direction of the dapper Mr Winstanley, who, at barely seventy-two, was regarded as young in their eyes, because, like Holmes, he was a confirmed bachelor, but had made a considerable fortune in the city, thus eminently desirable. He poured a cup of tea from the pot, being at pains to clarify what had excited his reason.

"Imagine, if you will, last Tuesday, upon a moonlit night, there was I in my gardening apron and gloves tending my plot, pouring a precise measure of water and liquid manure over my patch of plump, well-nourished marrows when, over the flinty churchyard wall, I see old Bantock from Lockbridge Manor hovering, as it were, before the venerable family tomb. Pardon me, the word 'hover' is probably a tad eccentric. Might I remind you, Herbert Bantock was interred the week before last, his funeral noted in the *Findon Times*."

"Yes, I read the obituary."

"You see, I was myself a pallbearer, supporting old Bantock's coffin into church. Common knowledge, family own the mill, and inn, the blacksmith's shop, three or four substantial houses and a good deal of land. I was invited to the funeral because he was a personal friend and fellow marrow grower, so no one should know better than me that he is dead and gone. But is he?"

"Quite, you infer this may have been old Bantock the ghost," said Holmes with wry amusement, putting down his cup.

"The facts?"

"I'd appreciate them".

"A grave shroud, the face wan and cadaverous, exactly like Bantock, the proximity of the family tomb, what other conclusion can there be? You see,

Holmes, I wonder why should old Bantock have chosen to rise from the grave? What disturbs his spirit? One realises that the committee, of which he was a past chairman, who oversees the judging of vegetable categories, will assemble on Saturday at ten to confer prizes. Might there be some cheating going on? Espionage planned? Say, one of my exceptional marrows fed a harmful concoction that could stunt its growth? Did his ghost appear to me as a warning?".

To Holmes, this proposal seemed unlikely. Ever tactful, he sought to offer friendly counsel. "You are *rightly* obsessed with your marrows at this time of season. The up-and-coming competition, the judging, the minutiae pressed upon you, but beware, beware, I say, of making a complete ass of yourself, Mr Winstanley. You could easily become a figure of ridicule if your views were to become common knowledge. I trust you have not told anyone else of old Bantock's ghost? Lower your voice, those women over there on the next table are known to be formidable gossips."

"Of course," said he, fully understanding. "I assure you, no other person, apart from ourselves, knows about this. Queer, damnably queer ..." he added reflectively.

"Go on."

"... Is how the ghost came to be smoking a pipe." Which reminded Holmes to take out his own pouch and forthwith light up his Austrian calabash pipe.

Still a joy to walk around the village – visit the church with its stained-glass windows, every amenity within easy distance – that afternoon, the heat at its zenith, Holmes chose to ride his Rover safety bicycle with Dunlop tyres, the intention being to briefly interview Mr Osmond, the local undertaker, wheelwright and general carpenter, at his yard where the hearse and horses were stabled.

Typically, Mr Osmond made field gates, wooden household items as well as coffins, both for the gentry and the commoner. He did very nicely out of this line of work. The fellow was busy in his yard stacking planks.

"Good day, Holmes, you won the golf, I hear, in partnership with who was it, John Watson?"

"Yes, we did. I wonder awfully, Mr Osmond, do you recall Sir Herbert Bantock's funeral, particularly what he was actually interred in? A shroud, sheeted?" he enquired.

Mr Osmond wiped his brow. "For the upper crust, best Sunday frock coat, pinstriped trousers, Lobbs shoes, hair done nice and tidy. 'Course, I dun 'im proud, with a stout oak coffin an' fittings, an' supplied the wagonette that took 'im on 'is final journey to the church."

"Oh, that's jolly well enough to be going on with," said Holmes lightly. "Thank you, Mr Osmond, good day."

So, what were the true circumstances concerning this ghost? He recalled the marrow-mad Mr Winstanley seemed convinced his vegetables were about to be sabotaged – hence the pistol – that the judging of the competition was fixed and he might miss out on the top prize. Then a breakthrough ... Holmes remembered his golfing win at the club, not just the

"Leaning the bike against rhododendron bushes along a wall"

gold cup, proudly put on the mantelpiece at Old Horseshoe Cottage, but two of the other contestants photographed in the local newspaper alongside he and Watson.

Keeping a stiff-backed posture, in a sprightly way, Holmes peddled his Rover up the gravel drive, thence informally leaning the bike against rhododendron bushes along a wall.

At a fair pace, he proceeded to enter the shady porch, the stonework carved with clawing griffins, central to the arch a hereditary coat of arms – certain the mystery of Old Bantock's ghost was finally in the bag. Holmes tugged the bell-pull and waited in the alcove. Not long after, the big nail-studded, banded door creaked ajar.

Peering at him in a kindly way was a little

crouched old lady with a hairy chin, in black mourning dress, wearing an old-fashioned lace cap and jet earrings. Holmes saw it was Agatha Welby, whom he remembered from the village jumble sales, manning the tea urn. She was a sprightly eighty-six and had served at Lockbridge Manor since a girl of fourteen.

"Why, Mr Sherlock Holmes isn't it? 'Ow's are yer, sir? Won the golf I read in the paper."

He instantly cut to the chase.

"Agatha, did you perchance see that picture in the *Findon Times* of Charlie and Reg Proogel – runners-up?"

"Arr, did too. Twins, the pair of 'em, known 'em as wee laddies that went to the schoolhouse."

"I surmise Sir Herbert Bantock, himself had a

twin, must have because someone jolly well saw him after he was meant to be dead."

"Where 'bouts?"

"Churchyard."

"Ooh saw 'im"

"Mr Winstanley from the clergyhouse."

The elderly retainer tittered, her violet eyes twinkling merrily. "Oh, 'im, dopey 'bout marrows, wants to marry one, I 'ears," the old woman chuckled. "Lor' bless yer, sir, yer sharp as a tack, an' no mistake. He ain't 'ere in this worl' n'more, course 'e ain't, but it were Sir Herbert's estranged brother from Yorkshire, Stan Bantock. What 'appened was this … in his last weeks on God's earth, up in 'is bed, still sensible in 'is mind, like, the master took pity on 'is 'arrogate sibling, who 'e 'ad not seen in years, and decides to pass on five-hundred pounds worth of cashable shares kep' private in 'is safe.

The will, o' course, were sacrosanct. All 'is money an' worldly goods to his wife, whom he loved dearly. Her Ladyship was never that keen on Old Stan, if yer gets my meanin'. She would've not left 'im a halfpenny, and none o' this shares, wotnot. She would 'ave gone to law if she 'ad ta. Well, Sir Herbert entrusted me, ol' Aggie, his devoted housekeeper, to hide them certificates in a place Her Ladyship an' the family solicitor was unlikely to find 'em. Even in his last days, how clever were the master? Lawks, he came up with a cracker. 'Aggy', he says, 'slip them valuable papers, deary, under me body afore the lid of the coffin gets screwed down. When I'm on show,' as he put it, 'in me best

Sundays.'

"Well, sir, I dun' right by 'im. I ain't got nuffink to be ashamed of. To cut a long story, when Her Ladyship went orf for a couple of days to see her sister, I telegraphed Stan and he comes down by express train, but I hid 'im from the servants, put Stan up in the attic with a mattress an' provisions, tols 'im to stay put, only go out at night, an' blow me, very late at night, 'e sneaks out to the ol' tomb, in e's nightshirt an' bedcap, a stub o' candle and a screwdriver 'andy, to claim what was 'is. The pong of that baccy Stan smoked in 'is pipe should 'ave given the game away to my way of thinkin'."

The Mews Mystery

The vicar of St Margaret's, over at Brambledean, the church long notable for its historical association with smugglers, called on Holmes one morning, thrusting an edition of the Parish magazine onto the breakfast table. Polishing off his ham and eggs, now in his eighties, the man feted in his time as the greatest detective of them all, perused the following notice, heavily underlined in green ink.

PARISH NEWS

Dear Parishioners,

Professor Simpkins, the eminent scientist, and his wife Peggy's dog went missing last week. Both devoted pet owners, if that were not bad enough, while involved in a frantic search their property was burgled, not only their own cottage, but that of Maud Marsh and Olive Tenberry, who also live in the Mews and joined the search party.

Typical of the police, they have drawn a complete blank, both for the incredible disappearance of the professor's dog, vanished into thin air. I can vouch a delightful Scotch terrier with the sweetest temperament, but also the missing valuables. Anyone with a smidgen of information on either count should forthwith contact me, the vicar or the church warden without delay. Professor Simpkins, as residents of our village will realise, is a member of our church committee. Of special mention, Major Waring was unstirringly selfless in his rapid organisation of a search party and spent considerable time, as did Mrs Jenkins, Maud Marsh, Olive Tenberry, Mr Crowfield, Mr Laughton, Mrs Lamb and her daughter

Ivy – scouring every inch of the village, including fields and the coastal path In a vain attempt to locate poor Minnie.

Our hearts go out to the professor and his wife, Peggy, and the other Mews residents, at this time of trial.

The Reverend Peter Armitage, MA (CANTAB)

"My dear Holmes," said the clergyman, lighting a cigarette. "I am bound to ask, with your assured reputation, even in retirement, if you will find time to investigate this most perplexing village matter. Seems to me those dullards, the rural police force, are simply procrastinating idiots. Now, if Scotland Yard were to take an interest, we might actually get somewhere. Don't you play golf occasionally with the Commissioner?"

"Unlikely, I am more of an historic figure these days. My influence should be limited within the structure, the organisation of the modern force. London is the metropolitan's true métier. Alas, the provinces suffer." Holmes pushed his plate aside helping himself to toast from the rack brought to the table by his home domestic, Mrs Cobbs, who poured fresh coffee for the gentleman prior to withdrawing to attend her other chores. "But your Mews mystery stimulates my interest."

"By heavens, Holmes, you'd really care to take on this village crime?"

"I think I will, the day's mine to seize, after all."

"And pray," the vicar drunk the remainder of his coffee, "I must enquire how your beekeeping progresses. Your hives prosper, I trust Sussex pure honey benefits from your cottage industry."

"I'm hardly the local bee expert, people will still ask me about that, I even get letters. What I say is, I'm afraid that particular pastime failed to engage me for long. To be honest, Peter, golf and reading are my real passions. That, and jumble sales and attending village concerts at the hall. I could not ask for better. Coastal walks with the dog, shopping in the village always a pleasure."

"You play Weber and Mendelssohn very passably. I and my wife were impressed with your musicianship. A Findon Christmas concert a few years back accompanied by Mrs Worth on pianoforte."

"You're too kind, alas arthritis encroaches upon my bow fingers. An expensive violin thus remains redundant in its case. But, back to the present. I can perhaps bring my past experience to bear on this Mews puzzle."

Breakfast finished, the vicar wearing long, belted leather coat, cap and goggles, drove Holmes over to Brambledean on his motorcycle and sidecar. Taking the fast route across the Downs.

A short walk from the great chalk cliffs, where sea birds circled, Holmes' cottage faced all the vicissitudes of the channel weather. For every day, he preferred rather dowdy, casual clothes. Kept upon one of his pegs an old Deerstalker hat. For now, he dug out his tough-wearing Inverness cape that he rarely wore, deemed entirely suitable by the vicar for travelling along roads at speed. Holmes' wilful golden Labrador certainly wanted to come along for the ride, having to be restrained from scrambling onto his master's lap.

Bidding his domestic a fond adieu, the retiree wisely tied the flaps of his hat extra tightly beneath his chin.

"I shall lay out a good meat tea for your return, Mr Holmes," she called from the honeysuckle porch.

"Thank you kindly, Mrs Cobbs."

The day was perfect, the sun pouring down. How the air flew past as viewed from the motorcycle sidecar of the cleric's smoky 500cc combination – post-and-wire fencing, dark hedges, the landscape lushly grassed with the sea beyond proved quite exhilarating.

The route that led into the village descended down a steep dip, an old grey-boarded smock windmill visible up near the golf course.

Emphasising Brambledean's quaint, pretty character, shops, houses and hostelries mostly half-timbered constructed mainly from local flint and rusty-red bricks. The narrow pavements on either side of the High Street laid out in patterns of flat, clay tiles.

Further along from the shops on the corner of Beach Road leading up towards the cliffs was the Mews. Four ancient, seventeenth-century cottages. Passing through the gate, introductions were made. The clergyman proving agreeable and friendly to his known parishioners and they too he. Although the residents seemed slightly wary of Holmes, for even in old age he remained tall, above average height, hawk-like and imposing.

The clay pots of flowering perennials, the climbing roses, the beautifully maintained gardens, each cottage with its individual post- box, in fact the entire square was ablaze with colour. The clipped hedges and greenery vital and gleaming. The eminent professor gathered round, so too his wife.

"Your vicar's meritorious article in the parish magazine informed me of the gist of the enquiry. Pray, let me hear it from yourselves. I know it's a bore after enduring interminable interviews with those thick-headed, rural police, but we'd better move forward. Who, pray, was robbed exactly, and of what?"

"We were," the scientist cleared his throat. "That is my wife lost her emerald brooch, Maud Marsh at number 1 her jewelled casket and Miss. Tenberry next door certain of her cabinet silverware. I might add, the old lady at number 4 across the way is rather hard of hearing and escaped this mass burglary.

"And your dog. The facts if you will. Forgive me, I like to dwell upon small insignificant details in particular."

"We believe the gate was left open, Minnie wandered out onto Beach Road and we've not seen her since, nor has she been reported run over." Mrs Simpkins said primly.

"Let us not be wholly naïve," Holmes proposed, unsmiling and taciturn. "Your dog, I think, was *deliberately* lured past the gate. That is my own conviction presented with the facts as they are. So, a search party was raised. You were joined by a group of concerned neighbours and friends, among them Major Waring, late of the India army – the main organising force."

"Absolutely, Mr Holmes, but I really can't agree our dog had anything to do with the burglary," said the professor warily.

"On the contrary," Holmes emphasised. "This was a deliberate ruse calculated to get you and the others out of the cottages. By someone, I hasten to say, well-known to you. And, above all, your dog went willingly without barking or making a fuss, that much is plain."

"A rattling good theory, Holmes," acknowledged the vicar, donning his goggles and motoring cap. "I'm bound to be off, I have to attend my parochial duties back at St Margaret's rectory. Stroll over

"The eminent professor gathered round, so too his wife"

when you want a lift back to Findon."

The gate clanged shut, Brambledean village, loud as ever with horse traffic, the odd car or solid-tyred motor-omnibus contributing to the din. Despite the clergyman's positivity, there were, nevertheless, doubts raised. The professor, for one.

"Deliberate? Well, I can't quite see that myself," said he, scratching his head. "The two incidents are linked, you say. No, can't see the connection."

"Oh poor Minnie," the wife sighed, seemingly as bemused as her husband, which irritated the retired detective who preferred to keep things sharp.

Never one to dodge the issue, old Mr Holmes was blunt and to the point. "I fear, Mrs Simpkins, you are unlikely to ever see your dog again. A quantity of the missing valuables may, if you are lucky, be recoverable by police if fenced, say, along Brighton lanes. I wish I could offer you more cheer concerning your pet, but there we are. Let us bring this ruthless crook to justice, as I intend doing. Well, well," Holmes attention got distracted. "Here is the little silver-haired old lady peeping her head round the front door of number 4, watching from the window earlier. Come, come, madam, we shan't bite."

"Mrs Wright, may I introduce Mr Sherlock Holmes who lives near Findon," Peggy said respectfully. "He's come to help make sense of the burglary."

The dignified, elderly lady, in her nineties, stooped somewhat by her great age, an alert twinkle in her eye only nodded. In her left hand she held up a shiny coin twixt fingers, waggling it at the scientist's wife.

"Am I missing something," requested Holmes, intrigued by the old woman's insistent gestures, but all was soon revealed.

"The window cleaning money, Peggy," the old lady exclaimed. "I forgot to pay Donald his regular sixpence when he last did our windows in the Mews. Forgetful, aren't I, but I am ninety- one, after all, and still quite active," she added somewhat conceitedly. "Us old uns don't have much use in modern society, I suppose, but there again ..."

"On the contrary," said Holmes, striking a match to his tobacco pipe, puffing furiously to get it going. "Us old uns do allow for something in society. Take yourself for instance, Mrs Wright. Why, you have just quite unwittingly provided me with the final piece of the jigsaw that shall bring a criminal to face the law."

"What's that, dear?" she cupped her hand to her ear.

"The stolen valuables, the dog's mysterious disappearance," Holmes shouted.

"Oh, I see."

"She's very hard of hearing, Mr Holmes," a bright, interested voice spoke up. Maud Marsh had been sunning herself in a deckchair listening to the ongoing conversation from behind the tall hedge. She proceeded to join the others in the square. "We call Mrs Wright 'The Queen of the Mews'," she went on to explain excitedly. "She's lived at number 4 simply forever, and in her time an integral part of village social life. Chairman of numerous committees, very capable at croquet."

"I confess," replied Holmes, "this little old lady has struck a chord. Why, gracious, a window cleaner is the perfect candidate and fits the burglar's profile exactly. A shrewd fellow up or down a ladder can, after all, keep a very close eye on the contents of your cottage both upstairs and below. Poised with his chamois leather and damp cloth wiping each pane well able to discern the layout intimately for each Mews cottage."

"Donald, the window cleaner?" Olive Tenberry was aghast, incredulous.

"The same. I have no hesitation in recommending he be arrested and his local lodgings searched at once."

"Nonsense, Donald is from the local firm of

Dunnington's – I trust him implicitly. He's done our windows since the beginning of the year," uttered an aggrieved Mrs. Simpkins.

"Exactly why he should be arrested. A brazen scoundrel if ever."

The wife appeared stunned.

"Getting emotional is all very well," answered Holmes, puffing on his pipe, trying to calm the wave of building resentment. "However, please don't allow this to cloud your better judgement. I repeat, the perpetrator of this burglary was well- known to you residents, and more importantly, your dog also! I cannot speak plainer. The Scottie remained passive throughout – no yapping, no commotion when lured onto Beach Road, then snatched – the gate conveniently left ajar."

"Yes, I recall our window cleaner visited us on that same day. We're normally very strict about the gate, you know the cliff path runs quite close." Maud had a growing awareness that Holmes might be right. "Was the latch checked?" she said out loud.

"Thereby, setting off a chain of circumstance. Donald well knew a search should ensue and the properties be left empty of residents. I shall now alert the vicar to my findings, thus he can shake those rural policemen into action. Drat, my pipe is out. Good day to you all." Sherlock Holmes raised his worn, old Deerstalker hat and departed searching frantically for his matches.

A Surfeit of Ice Cream

Mrs. Cobbs did for him cooking and cleaning, six days a week. She was good, too.

Holmes adored her dependable service and always paid her promptly from a tin that he kept forever on top of the Welsh dresser. A little blue tin labelled 'Edgeworth's Extra High Grade Sliced Pipe Tobacco'.

Just now, Mrs Cobbs was removing from the oven a wire tray full of current cakes. The smell wafting deliciously round the cottage. Holmes, himself, was attempting the *Times* crossword. His elderly Labrador recently washed in the tin tub sprawled before the fire guard. One of the words across – 'Neapolitan' - started him off on a queer chain of thought. He recalled that summer's morning, a week or so past, at the tearoom along the High Street, the door pinged and in waddled the bulky presence of Ken Albright, a local character known around and about Findon, recently married to the widow Mrs Ann Fenn from Peacehaven. Red-faced, wheezy, the considerably large fellow squeezed himself between tables, awkwardly manoeuvring his legs, thick as tree trunks across to the further window seat.

Watson had joined his old Baker Street comrade for a round of golf earlier. "Gracious," he remarked, sipping his Earl Grey, eyes twinkling merrily, "Ken is rather overweight. I don't recall him being so fat when I last saw him on the links."

"Indeed," replied Holmes. "Yes, he has rather put on the pounds."

Both he and Dr Watson watched with interest as the changed constitution presently parked over by the sunny window gave his order to the pretty waitress.

"A large helping of ice cream – the largest. No, wait, my dear, why not one of those delicious sundaes Jill is so famous for. Why, it is quite the weather, is it not?"

"Very well," answered Dora Dobson, writing it all down on a pad. "Anything else, Mr Albright?"

"Oh, a cup of tea," Ken dabbed his lumpen glistening forehead with a hanky, for it was indeed a warm, summer's day. Holmes was consuming a slice of jam sponge, but could not help but hear the wheezy, laboured breath. Watson, up for the day for a round of golf, unable to stem his curiosity, glanced up once more at Ken, spooning the ice cream into his wide-apart mouth with untold relish, flabby jowls trembling all the while.

"Another helping," he intimated to Dora, wiping his multitudinous chins with a table napkin. "My compliments to Jill, such sundaes were never created but by her."

"I shall pass on your kindness," said the waitress, smiling sweetly, knowing she was onto a good tip.

And so it was, Holmes and Watson, after paying the bill, gathering their golf clubs, quit the bustling tea shop – the good doctor stepping aside to allow a very prim, respectable, stick-thin lady to pass, who, it transpired, was none other than Ken's new wife of six months – Ann from Peacehaven. She entered the tea rooms and took her seat.

Mr Albright was a financial adviser, a partner in the village firm of Albright and Whitworth, so he was quite well off. Common knowledge, he met Ann at Sunday church where she had begun, all of a sudden to attend worship. She soon became a regular, as Holmes knew first-hand from the local vicar, with all the jumble activities, flower arranging and polishing brass duties. She was popular and valued.

Kenneth, also a member of the congregation, Holmes knew was, until then, a confirmed bachelor. A man happy in his own company, seemingly knocked for six by cupid's arrow, for he and Ann were soon courting amusing his friends and financial clients alike by announcing a surprise engagement. The chap had been thinner then – still a large-built man, but in no way the burgeoning fatty he was to become.

This matter of Mr Albright renewed itself when Holmes happened to bump into Ken stepping out of his High Street offices one Tuesday. "You certainly do love your ice cream, Mr Albright, so do I. Strawberry is my favourite." He said this, not in a condescending way, for there was purpose behind the remark.

"Oh, do you Holmes? Y'know," he sighed, "my darling wife Ann insists I enjoy a portion at lunch, dinner and tea, so can't complain."

All of a sudden, Ken grimaced, assaulted by a

severe pain in his chest. He steadied himself against a wall. After a sharp intake of breath, he muttered feebly, "Indigestion, better get some powders from the pharmacist." Holmes noted how the chap had rapidly gained weight since his marriage. "No more than indigestion." He heard him mutter while crossing the road.

Putting his folded newspaper aside, abandoning seven across – two down, Holmes enquired of his domestic, always up on local gossip – to reveal certain details.

"Mrs Cobbs, what did Ann Fenn's first husband die of? Was it in the papers? The funeral was, of course, mentioned in the *Findon Times*."

"What a queer question, Mr Holmes. A heart failure if I remember correctly. Still but middle-aged – quite young really. At the last coffee morning, I was having a natter. Mrs Kemp mentioned his sudden death, collapsing at the office. He was a solicitor over at Peacehaven and very popular. It all came as quite a shock. Kenneth, bless him, helped perk her up again, lift her out of her grief. Ken adores her, *it's a match made in heaven* according to the vicar."

"Ken and Ann, I grant you, do look the happy couple," said Holmes, lighting his pipe. "Although," he cautioned, "is it too good to be true – a bit on the rebound? I'm never quite sure whether that's a good thing. Watson tells me women are awfully vulnerable after the passing of a spouse. I do hope the newly-weds remain content. Was he very large, then?" he added.

"Who was large? To whom are you referring?"

asked Mrs Cobbs, somewhat petulantly.

"Oh, nothing." Might there indeed exist the possibility, despite the outward show of marital bliss, murder was being done. Holmes felt seized more than ever, by a need to pry, to question. Certainly, Ken's health was deteriorating, seemed to be addicted to ice cream, ice cream available at the local shop, the tea rooms and, no doubt, prepared at home in metal snap together moulds by Mrs Kemp, the Albright's devoted housekeeper. So sure was he of malicious intent on the part of the wife, he hastened to the police house to visit Sergeant Sturmer to test a theory, but was it all just silly nonsense! An old fellow sticking his nose in where he shouldn't! Retired now from years of consulting work, he required a sounding board, a person well-versed in the clever wiles of the criminal mind.

"Your idea takes a bit of getting used to," said the

"Another helping, he intimated to Dora"

officer, puffing on his tobacco pipe, trying his best to take the old man seriously. "Let's look at this from a logical angle. You infer that Ken is being deliberately murdered by his wife, Ann, the former widow Ann Fenn whom you suspect is poisoning him by stuffing him with ice cream at every opportunity. That he has now become a hopeless addict, unable to resist portions?"

"I am," replied Holmes confidently. "And something must be done, otherwise, poor, unsuspecting Mr Albright may die. Oh, I know it's only an idea, but can't you find out the exact circumstances of her previous husband's death. I mean, if he is in harm's way, better to act."

The policeman nodded. "The coroner, Mr Edwards, might help, or there's the late solicitor's medical practitioner over at Peacehaven."

"When did he pass away, Sergeant?"

"Last spring, the local papers took note of the funeral. But, blazes, this is just too daft for words. We all of us partake of ice cream from time to time. Ice cream as a method of murder? I should be laughed out of the county constabulary, jeered out of the force."

But still, the old man Sherlock Holmes remained persistent.

A week later, a heatwave in progress, Mrs Cobbs was busy in the kitchen at Horseshoe Cottage. She prepared Holmes a cooling glass of barley water to take outside into the sunny garden.

"Ken Albright has been admitted to hospital," she said. "Mrs Albright's been arrested, arrested, think of it. Everyone in the village is talking about it. Y'know, she apparently insisted each of her husbands take out enormous insurance policies. There's even been a suggestion a body is to be exhumed over at Peacehaven. Just too awful. One of her husbands, they suspect, was poisoned by arsenic!"

"The other nearly by a surfeit of ice cream," replied Holmes, coming in from the sunny patio, bearing his clippers, wryly glancing at Mrs Cobbs who gave a wistful smile in return.

Frightening how perceptive that man is, she thought.

Train to West Grinstead

Holmes dug out the framed pen-and-ink drawing covered with dust from underneath the sofa where it had lain for years, thence propped it against cushions and called out for his domestic, Mrs Cobbs, presently at the range cooking luncheon to come and have a look at it.

"Your view, Mrs Cobbs, be honest. Should I keep or chuck it out to the jumble?"

The tubby, rosy-cheeked woman stood her ground, wiping her hands down the front of her pinny.

"Well, now, it's a rushing waterfall," she declared, cocking her head to one side. "But, no, no, I'd say not a bad picture. Try that emporium in

Henfield, worth better than the jumble sale. Someone's sure to buy it. Very dramatic an' the frame's tidy, like. 'Ere, I'll give it a proper dust. George Green'll provide you with a bit of cash anyhow."

"Well, yes, George's quite fair with money. Y'know, I believe you're right, Mrs Cobbs. The emporium at Henfield it is, then."

Pausing to light his Austrian calabash pipe, he thought this a capital solution.

———

The emporium, or Greens, as it was known locally, was a most excellent, large store along the High Street, selling all manner of high quality bric-a-brac, including a good selection of secondhand books. Sometimes, on his way to Horsham, to visit

Watson, he would spend time browsing, having picked up some nice brass ships lanterns for his downland cottage.

"Hello, Mr Holmes, what's that brown paper package tucked under your arm. Here, let me untie it."

"These leftover pieces from my Baker Street days, George. I just haven't the room. Watson used to have an acute interest in owning this picture, but even that waned over our years of retirement."

"Horsham, isn't it? You both won the golf I read in the paper. Your eye must still be sharp."

"Yes, he lives there with a lady friend, Mrs Eden, herself seventy-three years young."

"Oh, Reichenbach Falls, well I never." Mr Green, admired the framed picture. "When we were younger, I passed through that same region which must hold so many memories for you. My future wife and I were on a hiking tour – nice hotel. Sure you want to pass on such an iconic picture? Could go to auction, you know, what with the provenance."

"No, I am resolved. My domestic, Mrs Cobbs, gave the final verdict. So much Baker Street clutter."

"Alright, Mr Holmes, I'll take it off your hands. What's up ...!" the proprietor noticed the long-retired consulting detective seized by curiosity stooped over a cardboard box full of oddments, yet to be classified, dumped beside his desk. That unfailing alert eye had spotted something.

"How much for this calf-bound Latin dictionary?" asked the masterful observer of countless minutiae, raising himself to his full height.

"Cover's damaged, binding torn – still of fair quality. Belonged to somebody's library, I shouldn't wonder. I've yet to value the box's contents. Say two shillings. There's better books, y'know."

"Done."

All the way home on the motorbus, Holmes' excitement was palpable. He even found himself acknowledging the smiles of certain elder lady passengers. Gazing out of the bus window, he hummed snatches of Sarasati, else Mendelssohn. Alas, the ability to play this dazzling array of melodies now somewhat hampered by arthritis.

Having walked the familiar upward slope from the village to a place adjoining a chalk ridge track leading across the Downs to his cottage, Holmes', silver-topped cane in hand, was greeted at the honeysuckle porch by his barking Labrador – Mrs Cobbs, around the back, tending not to an apiary, but rather the hen coop. The dog went through to the parlour flopping in a heap on the Turkey rug.

Meanwhile, the retiree, overcome with an exuberant sense of intuition that rarely failed him, flung his stick in the blue and white vase employed as a first-rate umbrella stand just inside the stable door. Thence, he dashed across to his desk, making a grab for a magnifying lens, focusing on the front cover of the second-hand dictionary laid uppermost against the blotter. His examination proved purposeful. He meticulously took account of each of the various tares on the leather-embossed cover. Opening the dictionary, he already knew a thick volume of pages alike pierced, in some cases, to a depth of three inches or more by a sharp implement.

The tares, he surmised, the result of a violent stabbing motion, say from a large knife. During the Baker Street years, he had encountered similar marks – for instance, the wounds of a recent murder victim kept at the mortuary. Anyhow, whoever struck the book in this way did so forcefully.

Fanning the pages, he observed the Ex-libris gummed sticker had at some stage been removed. A small pencil notation existed on the corner of a page. This Latin dictionary showed promise – suppose somebody reading, browsing its pages, say, had suddenly been attacked unawares, forced by circumstance to block the blows, fending them off with this thick Latin volume, using it as an impromptu defensive shield.

No doubt good old Watson should scoff at his primary deductions – but not for long, he chuckled. This was all leading somewhere, he felt sure of that.

Mrs Cobb returned from attending to the fowls and set a cup of tea beside him. He chose a pipe from the rack and took his time filling it with Ogden's Sliced Cobnut Tobacco – the mellower brand he favoured these days.

"Oh, good Lord, what brings you back to my shop so quickly? Not going to quibble about the price of that old Latin book, surely? I trust my reputation remains unsullied," Mr Green joked.

"Quite the contrary, I find myself indebted to the

old dictionary's shabby condition, the state of it's cover. George, please tell me that cardboard box still awaits your sifting and pricing. Are all the objects d'art still intact?"

"Objects d'art – leave over, Mr Holmes. Mostly junk. As a matter of fact, I shoved the box behind this curtain. Nothing much of value, nor interest – carving knife, seen plenty of those before, bone-handled fish set, cheap china service, salt and pepper pots – below my range, I'm afraid."

"But not mine – may I?"

"Certainly, the fish knives you can have for sixpence – they are engraved."

Sherlock Holmes lost no time emptying the contents on the table. Removing the bulky, Latin dictionary from his haversack, he picked up the carving knife inserting the blade into one of the tares, defacing the book's front cover. Sliding the blade further, he found it fitted exactly. More of the same followed until he felt in no doubt this was the knife, these marks sustained by a chosen weapon.

"Might I enquire who brought the box into the shop?"

"A Mrs Worthy and a Mrs Clarke. I was pressed for time and advised them to pop in next week, and that if I wanted to buy anything I should pay them then. The ladies agreed."

"Local?"

"They didn't say."

Holmes turned his attention to examining the other bric-a-brac. Of major interest, a discarded stub of a return ticket to West Grinstead found in the

"Sliding the blade further, he found it fitted exactly"

bottom of the box.

West Grinstead was a stop on the Steyning Line operated by the London, Brighton & South Coast Railway. How was it, Henfield, Steyning, Partridge Green, Southwater Brickworks... something like that. He'd personally taken the train dozens of times over the years to reach Horsham – Watson's destination, and he was about to take the passenger service again.

That very afternoon, boarding the train, the long-retired consulting detective took out his pouch of Ogden's Cobnut Sliced tobacco, filling his pipe and lighting the mixture. He smoked for a while, gazing out of the compartment window at the passing scene. The countryside delightful at this time of season. From Steyning, the slow stopping service rattled gently along the Adur valley, Chanctonberry Ring, the famous landmark atop of the hill, the treeline visible in the distance as they rounded the curve. Next was Henfield, thence the branch line led towards Partridge Green.

Alighting at West Grinstead, amid the low-lying Weald, Holmes took a leisurely stroll to St George's church. Architecturally pleasing, possessed of a broach spire, and fourteenth- century timber porch. However, it was the rectory, a pleasant old, red-brick house covered in creepers that he turned to. Long known to him, the public house, else the vicarage, always a wonderful source of local information, nay gossip.

"Vicar, might I have a word?"

"My dear fellow, is it about that funeral – Miss Lacy, is to be buried tomorrow at eleven. We expect a good turnout and a first-rate tea in the village hall after. Some ladies, Mrs Worthy and Mrs Clarke and Miss Southwick from my church cleaned out her cottage on Tuesday. A distant relative?"

"Hardly." Holmes smiled. "Do you perchance recognise this Latin dictionary? To my mind, although in a vandalised state, once a rare and valuable volume, belonging to, I hazard to say, a retired scholar, an antiquarian, a bibliophile possessed of a well-loved library collected over many years. Perhaps from university days. I enjoy reading myself, and share something of an affinity with these tatty old second handers – don't you?"

"Indeed, sir," the vicar replied rapturously. "I am myself devoted to the joys of searching out literary gems, early editions of Smollet in Alfriston or Brighton – gracious heavens!" the clergyman exclaimed, raising his tufty eyebrows, "You know, I place this dictionary you present me to the late Mr Crawford at Ninfield House. The main factor, see the little pencil number on the right, upper corner of the frontispiece. That is a personal mark, the fellow's academic achievements exactly as you describe. You must have heard about it – no? Well, perhaps not, so long ago."

"I congratulate you on your precise observations," answered Holmes with a thin smile. "Pray, enlighten me further."

"The chap, you see, was unfortunately murdered – dead – Marrat in the bath springs to mind."

"Stabbed?"

"A violent attack, I am told, but this happened many years ago – way back. My predecessor, Reverend Clagthorn mentioned the event. Certain of the villagers remember, of course. You see, the police never did find out who killed him. The case remains to this day a mystery. Pretty much forgotten – maybe for the best. The village was notorious, from morbid sightseers. That state of affairs lasted for a year or more. Mr Crawford's lovely Georgian house 'Ninfield' became infamous, drawing the wrong sort of tourists."

"Well, the wrong or the right sort spend money at the shops and pubs, don't they?"

"True, true – suppose you're right Mr..."

"Holmes. I'm about to become a morbid tourist myself."

"Mr Crawford's house," the vicar laughed raucously. "His brother, who inherited the library, and his wife live there now. Delightful couple. I don't expect they'll let you look around. Queer, Miss Lacy, who is being buried tomorrow, was Mr

Crawford's housekeeper."

"Now that interests me, significantly so."

Regarding the imposing tanned stranger in the Breton cap and blazer quizzically, the vicar nodded, taking out his case of cigarettes proffering one, Holmes refusing.

"We in the village, nay, on the entire estate, even the gentry at the big house knew her to be a kind, generous and God-fearing woman, although her acquired fame was more of a hindrance. Quite naturally, for the rest of her life, she was reticent to explain the true horror of that crime."

"Miss Lacy, I'll be bound, first to discover the body and reported the incident promptly."

"She did. Cooperated fully with the police, but afterwards preferred not to talk of it! Such terrible circumstances, what must have been the shock of finding her master like that?"

Else involved in actually killing him, thought Holmes cynically, utterly convinced Miss Lacy was the clever killer who had escaped punishment all these years.

"And she lived where?"

"Why, along the lane."

"Alas, I must catch my train and put off the pilgrimage, but you have been most helpful."

The clergyman hesitated. "That Latin dictionary I am certain belonged to the late Mr Crawford, although it's shabby condition, I fear, Mr Holmes, predisposes it to either be mended at fair expense, or got rid of."

How many times had Holmes travelled this same

route along the branch to visit friend Watson? He twisted his mouth into a smile, and today, West Grinstead, just a rural village usually passed with vague interest had become a place memorable for a crime. Yet, as he surveyed the pleasant, Wealden landscape, he took a radical decision.

Let the woman be decently buried at St George's, her secret go to the grave with her, he vowed to himself, lighting his pipe. Leaning forward on the cloth-covered seat. *I'm just too old to go harassing the police to reopen the case. I'd rather be on the links. Good old Watson might appreciate this little West Grinstead foray.* Pipe in mouth, he lifted the Latin dictionary out of his haversack flinging it with surprising strength out of the partly-opened carriage window, so it fell amongst the track-side foliage. *Lost forever, gone and*

"Holmes took the train."

good riddance. Let the past rest easy he concluded as the train clattered onwards.

Mr Crawford murdered over what? A dispute, some passionate intrigue turned sour, a change to his will, a refusal to raise her salary after years of devoted service. Whatever, some matter tipped Miss Lacy into an uncontrollable rage, causing her to stab him to death. She kept the book and the knife all these years, knowing it was valuable evidence that could link her to a heinous crime – even unto old age.

The Bird Table Thief

Preceding a substantial fall of snow during the latter stages of the night, tiled roofs and lintels and gardens of homesteads on the Downs were blanketed white. Such were the freezing temperatures up there an array of icicles clung in profusion to the gutters and drainpipes.

A loud rap, that wintry morning on the stable door of Horseshoe Cottage, heralded a visitor. About to pour coffee from the pot, Mrs Cobbs hurriedly went to answer its summons. The breakfast table was laid just as Holmes preferred – a pat of farm butter, rack full of wholemeal toast, a pot of chunky Oxford marmalade, plate heaped with ham and eggs. As good a breakfast as any householder in England could wish for.

The schoolhouse in the village, being closed for the foreseeable future, the weather so severe meant, brilliantly, children would not attend classes, but visit friends to skate on ponds or join in tobogganing.

Who then, was the visitor? It was Sally Sudbury from the neighbouring cottage, the woman practically at her wits end. Offered a rush-seated chair close to the range, and a steaming cup of coffee by Mrs Cobbs, she blurted out her woes. Holmes, somewhat irritated, listened patiently enough tucking into his breakfast.

"For the last couple of days, I goes out to the bird table see, puts out the scraps of bread, crumbled cake, nuts and suet and, lawks, no sooner is me back turned – gorn! Them poor weeny robins, tits and sparrows deprived of their right to a proper meal. It just won't do, Mr Holmes. See starlings be the bullies. *Wot a mess they do make*, but it ain't starlings. They arrive in February as a rule. Now, there's Mr and Mrs Blackbird, the robins and their wives, Mr and Mrs Sparrow, the blue and great tits – wot's to become of 'em if this cold spell lasts? Wot mayhap must they think of me? Six inches of snow on the ground – trees frozen with ice – no grub!"

Holmes replete, pushed back his plate and lit his pipe.

"I trust you are not about to accuse a snowman of straying into your garden and gobbling all the bird food. I think he must take severe umbrage at such a suggestion, Sally." Holmes smiled thinly at his domestic help, Mrs Cobbs. However, the light-hearted jokiness was lost on the woman – one female's devoted concern for the other.

"The problem, Mr Holmes, is the blessed privet hedge. Obscures my view of the bird table somewhat from the kitchen window – who be the villain, I wonder?"

"A stoat," suggested Holmes, puffing on his pipe, desperate to get on and read the newspaper and the woman to leave. Watson was always better at handling this sort of semi-hysterical appeal.

"Might be up to mischief, certainly."

"Weasel."

"Dunnosomuch."

"Grey squirrel – but I don't think we have any round here. A fox possibly." Sally quickly warmed to the topic of grey squirrels.

"When I lived in Larchford, we had squirrels come in from the woods – o' they're clever alright. One year, I chucked my Wellington boot at one of 'em to keep them from pestering the bird table. Made no difference – them squirrels scamper up a tree gazing down at you like you're the stupidest fool on earth. But you got me thinking, Mr Holmes. Why not don your deerstalker, 'n bring that famous magnifying wotsit of y'orn round to my garden."

"Well, I'm actually retired from detective work," he laughed. "My Baker Street days are long behind me. However, if you insist, Sally, I'm walking the dog later anyhow. I wonder if I should fetch good old Watson, over from Horsham, for backup."

Whilst Sally Sudbury headed home, doing the

washing up, Mrs Cobbs commented, "We've had heaps of coal stocked in the cellar, that's entirely due to taking our coal merchant's advice back in October when he predicted, as did many village folk, a harsh winter, because of the abundant fruiting berries along the hedgerow, particularly of holly."

The snowy conditions had indeed preserved a number of useful prints round by the bird table. Sally, arms crossed over her bosom, looked on while the long-retired consulting detective crouched stiffly with his lens. Holmes' Labrador sniffing round by the privet.

Facts to firstly consider were the birds, whose territory consisted of Sally's garden. Robins, tits, sparrows and blackbirds were ferociously efficient feeders. The birds, he supposed, could simply hop over the wall to his own cottage if they wanted to. But it was true, the ground was solid. The weather set to get colder. It was fascinating to wonder how long in these frozen conditions he himself, an elderly man, would last, could survive if shrunk down to the size of a robin, forced to fend for himself. All those carnivorous birds and prowling animals, only too glad of an easy meal. Quite suddenly, his magnifying lens revealed an exciting discrepancy which he must follow up. Next port of call, then, was the cliffs, but a short distance along the footpath from Horseshoe Cottage.

Despite the tough going, due to drifting snow, he and his dog soon enough managed to reach Cora Honeysett's home, one of a line of coastal cottages, and tugged the bell pull. No answer, he scanned the roof and chimney pots – no smoke. He was after local information, and none was better than Cora to supply it. As luck would have it, Miss Walsh from next door, a woman in her forties, was laying hearth cinders from a bucket onto her paved path. Beyond the cliffs could be heard waves crashing along the shingle beach. Holmes pressed home the data he had gleaned by earlier use of his magnifying lens, mostly used nowadays for combating annoyingly small print in works of fiction.

"Mrs Walsh," said he, leaning on his stout ash stick, "when I'm out walking my dog, I sometimes see 'old fox' out and about early, expectant of his breakfast egg. Nimble as can be, raiding the gulls' nests along that most perilous section of cliff."

"How 'e does patter along so daintily wi' his four

paws 'orn them ledges be remarkable," agreed the woman, pausing with her cinder bucket.

"Talking of sea birds, I wonder if you've ever seen a one-legged gull hereabouts – does such a species exist. Cora would be bound to know, wouldn't she?"

"'Fraid the old dear's gone by train to visit her son Steven for a week – Kentish way. I keeps an eye on her place for her, like – oh, there she is," cried Mrs Walsh, enthralled by the sighting of something in the dull grey sky, not, of course, an airborne Cora. "Suzanne, the one-legged gull. Maybe she'll land for us."

Sure enough, on cue, the seabird skimmed down settling on Mrs Walsh's tiled roof near the chimney pots. This encouraged her to elaborate further.

"Settling on Mrs Walsh's tiled roof near the chimney pots"

"Now, the story be this, Mr Holmes, unbeknown to thee, Cora fed the gull since she were a tiny chick every morn', wi'out fail. The seabird is rightly remarkable, for she breeds each year normal like, an' looks after her young brood despite bein' lame. Gets about very nicely, ta, but lawks, what a mess them gulls make of our roofs and chimney pots, an' the top o' street lamps, droppin' it orn our heads, ruinin' 'airdos."

So Holmes understood this eminently sensible gull, presently perched on Mrs Walsh's roof, after having fed very nicely at Sally Sudbury's bird table, had returned to her usual provider, her main source since a chick. Cora Honeysett, away in Kent, visiting her son. Hence, the raiding.

Having gleaned this intelligence, Holmes went

straight away back to his client to inform her of the bird table thief's true identity. Thus, she had best put up with more raiding in the near future until Cora's return.

Fumes of Saphir Médaille d'Or

Shaking itself, the Labrador forthwith flopped down on the rug. Lunch over, elderly Mr Holmes stretched himself languidly upon the sofa. Through the open-weave nets poured wintry sunshine making the brasses round the fireplace gleam. Filling his pipe, the retiree chose his tobacco jar, not the oily black shag of yore, but a milder mixture first recommended him by the local vicar in those far-off days of keeping bees – *Ogden's Cobnut Sliced*.

Placed on the side table next to him lay a partly-opened tin of Saphir Médaille d'Or, slightly warmed on a spirit lamp – a poor substitute for cocaine, yet still able, from the fumes when inhaled with pipe smoke, to induce a modest bout of euphoria. Picking up his Kenneth Graham novel, he found his bookmark, thus, whilst reading and smoking, started to pleasantly hallucinate.

Wiping a kitchen shelf that afternoon, the housekeeper recognised a gentle snoring coming from the sitting room. Always respectful, she thought better than disturbing her employee's slumberous state. After feeding the hens and refilling the coal scuttle, she would take Mr Holmes a pot of Brazil coffee to perk him up – for now, Mrs Cobbs gazed out of the kitchen window watching a pair of walkers taking the South Downs route, noting also the profusion of gulls swooping and diving above the cliffs – a portent of stormy weather ahead – the channel wind already picking up, the washing on the line leading a merry dance.

No sooner did Mr Badger quit his comfortable underground chambers, filled with winter stores, host to every bachelor convenience imaginable, locking the front door formed in a gnarled chestnut tree trunk, than he felt inclined to dither, questioning his intent to sally forth so early into the wild wood, now brittle with frost, branches icicle draped, patchy snow underfoot.

"None of this fuss pottin' and humbuggin', off yer go," he said to himself.

Twenty minutes later, plodding ankle deep in snow round a bend of hedgerow trees, his goal was more defined – to seek out his old chum on the matter of a recent local crime. He who resided on the lower reaches of an entrancing stream damned up in several places – overlooked by a most pleasingly situated weather-boarded cottage.

"Halloa, anyone at home?" he cried gruffly, slapping his gloved paws together.

Net curtains quivered, a female hedgehog, possessing an affable, prickly face, was glimpsed at a lower window. This being the housekeeper, Mrs Quill.

"Beaver," Badger yelled, throwing his scarf over his shoulder, the animal aware of a distinct plop-plopping.

Not long after the ice of the lower pond crackled apart. Mr Beaver, awash with ripples, surfaced from his morning dip, causing his friend consternation.

"How you can swim in that damnably cold murk at this time of season confounds me utterly," said the genial brock. "Wrong, all wrong – you'll catch a death."

"Now, now, a cold water dip first thing keeps a fella sharp. Invigorates the system. You should try it some time."

"Not bally likely."

The friends climbed steps that led to the quaint riverman's homestead.

Once inside Beaver's abode, the warmth from the range was a welcome contrast to the freezing, cloying damp of the engineered water channels without.

"Take the armchair, why don't you old chap. Toast yer paws in front of the hearth."

"So long as there's plenty of winter stores, a good log fire, all is well with the world. Y'know Beaver ..."

Mr Badger was all of a sudden struck dumb. The

most enticing smell of sizzling bacon filled the roomy residence. Mrs Quill presently frying ham and eggs in a pan, humming to herself. The animal's stripy snout sniffed appreciatively. "You will be staying for breakfast, I take it." Mr Beaver grinned, towelling himself down before slipping into his mousy-grey dressing gown.

"Rather. Nothing like a hearty breakfast to set a man up for the day. Now, what was I going to say? Ah, the *duck murders*, did you read the reports in the papers?"

"Certainly did." Beaver peered into the oval mirror, raking his bristly forehead with Taylor's lime cream. After, he dabbed his chops with Floris No.89, a must for any discerning gentlemen of the river.

"Massacre – nine ducks ab*duck*ted from Mr Toad's egg-laying shed, violently murdered – beheaded. They should have felt secure in their home."

"Yah, the egg-production plant murder sort of overshadowed that nature article about Mr Otter's work with the environment agency to increase fish stocks and maintain a clean water supply – that's our real world. Still, what was it? 'The most gruesome, ghastly crime ever, by far the worst for years'. The murders, a cause for much morbid speculation."

"An Inspector Trent, plodder through the grades, only just promoted, put in charge," sighed the brock incredulously. "Blast it all, y'know this duck caper is right up your street, Beaver. Toad wants someone on the ball, able to think. What the hell use is an official detective inspector?"

"*Defective* Inspector more like."

"Ha, how very droll," chuckled the mammal in full agreement. "Rural coppers are alright for flag waving a motor, sorting out a drunk, disorderly stoat, but really, something serious."

"Righ' ho, old friend." Beaver glanced in the oval mirror, pleased with his appearance. "Now, 'cordin'to the local papers, Toad runs a profitable sideline selling ducks' eggs locally. Mr Regis, the estate manager, does all the hard graft, of course."

"It is our duty to offer support and pop over to Toad Hall after brekky."

"Capital idea, Ah, while we've been gassing, Mrs Quill, bless her, rustled up a feast. Creamed porridge an' prunes, ham an' eggs, and grilled tomatoes, toast drippin' with farmhouse butter. By Jove, Badger, demolish away."

Thus, getting down to the serious business of eating, the animals ate heartily.

Smoking their after-breakfast pipes, either side of the hearth, a sullen menial entered the parlour. "You wanted me, guv." A teenage hedgehog in grubby work overalls, cap in claw, stood awaiting orders.

"Your bloomin' hobnail boots are spreading leaf mould all over my Wilton carpet," barked Mr Beaver. "Hurry up an' coal the steam launch AURORA. Come on laddy, Lor." He groaned as an aside to his friend. "The effort required to get this lot off their backsides in winter." Beaver leant his bulk forward to knock the ashes of his pipe out on the fender. "What impudence. That young fella has the audacity to ask me for a new wheelbarra and higher wages. What's society coming to?"

From the lower reaches, the riverbank a mass of speckled frosty foliage, the steam launch chugged reliably upstream, attaining Toad Hall around midday.

A constable approached the creek – the red - brick half-timbered Tudor house visible beyond the topiary. The officer saluted, helping tie and secure the steam craft to the jetty.

"A culprit still at large."

"Eh, no sir, we've arrested a suspect."

"Who's that then?" asked Badger doubtfully.

"Mangie ol' fox. By rights should be in the workhouse. Vagrant, slob, worthless dosser – ol'

Carteby. Know 'im? Tented illegally on Mr Toad's land – been conveyed to the lock-up. Them vagrants should all be hanged in my humble opinion. Necks snapped – kindest way, ain't it, sir?

"No, it's not," seethed the brock, a tad indignantly. "Takes all sorts to make a world."

"Ahem," Beaver announced. "Constable, I shall require to visit the scene of the murders. The duck hatchery – pronto! I am here at the specific request of Mr Toad – the Lord of the Manor."

"I'll take you both straight over, gents. Ah, Mr Beaver," said he, recognising the familiar attire of deerstalker, the Inverness cape of a rough twill, "I expect you brought along your magnifying lens, tee hee."

"Indeed, what do you find so amusing?"

"Yeah, like I says, ol' Carteby's your man. Gawd, 'es mange, but if the fox chooses to live life on the open road, what does he expect."

"A fair trial," thundered Badger. "Innocent 'til proven guilty in a court of law. Where's the inspector?" he barked irritably.

"Down the pub, 'aving 'is lunch, o' course."

Further on beyond the walled kitchen garden lay a patch of land given over to a number of production hatcheries. One of the huts had been broken into. Mr Toad, presently wearing his camel-haired overcoat, jodhpurs and an older motoring cap ruminated on all the blood and feathers spread about, plus his lost profits. The cost of replacing those fowls. But he did not remain gloomy for long.

"Hello you lot," said he, brightening up upon the

animals' approach. "Glad everso that you're wading in. I mean, old Carteby smells to high heaven, but always bin courteous to me personally. In summer, goes round the countryside, don't he, selling tat from a buckled pram. I thought the police rather heavy-handed earlier – didn't want to make a fuss, mind."

"The aged, mangy fox is toothless. Am I the only person to observe," the aquatic mammal sighed.

"What's that you say?"

"Well," Beaver searched for his pipe and matches. "y'know my domestic, Mrs Quill, charitable sort, last time the old mangy fox visited my house selling old tat, took pity and fed him round by the kitchen from my groaning larder. Reduced to soggy bread, bit of warm milk, cat food

– honestly, that's all he could eat. Forget cold mutton, lamb chops or, more pertinently, wriggling live prey – see, that should be the devil's own job to get his gnashers round – he hardly owns any teeth to speak of. Mind you, the old fox be devious enough."

"How's that?"

"Managed to squirrel away Mrs Quill's best bone-handled silver serving spoon, and other cutlery went missing on the last occasion he called."

"Thief, eh?"

Intrigued by this travelling crook, Toad leant back on his natty shooting stick, folding his arms. "Funny, the inspector was of the opinion the mange may have spread to the old fox's brain, affecting his behaviour, turning Carteby loopy. Logical enough theory, fit of uncontrolled aggression leads to wilful murder – SEEING RED. What about it?"

"Ahem, old Carteby?" sighed Mr Beaver. "I mean, honestly, Toad, the dead laid before us, were obviously shaken violently, duck breasts punctured by sharp fangs, a strong jaw at work here. Gripping prey. See my point?"

"Pardon me, Beaver," replied Toad, "but a veritable orgy or violence seems to have taken place, my prize egg-layers awfully set upon. Never stood a bloomin' chance. I'd guess more than one intruder involved?"

"We're certainly dealing with killing-for-killing's sake. Nothing remotely related to hunter-gatherers."

"If not old Carteby, then who?" Badger

conjectured, puffing on his pipe.

His friend was quick to respond.

"Maybe *wild wooders*. Beg pardon, Badger, excluding yourself, of course. But, as Toad I'm sure will verify, Alfie Ferret, Johnny Stoat, else the weasels, do have a reputation. Dodgy types to a man."

Each duck's corpse came in for minute scrutiny. Smartly turned out in his deerstalker, combined with a fetching Inverness cape of rough twill, Mr Beaver held a strong magnifying lens in his paw, searching for something important overlooked – a useful clue. He closely considered piles of feathers, the bloodied, decapitated corpses recently unearthed from shallow graves by police, the vicinity of the crime was scoured reverently. Thence, lastly, the duck hatchery itself. Grunting and sniffing, muttering all the while, 'no human agent here'.

He concluded they were looking for a predatory animal fond of blood sports.

Toad, considerate as always, beckoned in the direction of his magnificent home, offered a warm blast of fire and a stiff whisky to his dear chums, unable to cope with the idea of them being too long outside half freezing to death on his behalf. Anyhow, the light was fading, snow falling steadily – time to be indoors. Toad's munificent heart reached out even to the frozen policeman on duty.

"Hoppit, constable, go to the kitchen. Cook'll see ya alright – bit of damson cake, hot tea – inspector's down the pub anyhow, so he won't care."

"Very kind of you, sir. You eeze a real gentleman. Them dead ducks ain't about to run off, is they? Come on, Tom," grinned the sergeant, not one for hanging about. He, leading his fellow officer across the snowy lawn to the big house.

Latticed windows gleamed invitingly. Indeed, as darkness fell, anyone who had any sense headed that way.

Served a most excellent repast at long table, beneath the venerable oak roof beams and candelabrum of the great hall, the friends, well-fed and watered, adjourned to the library, shelves stacked full of pristine calf-bound volumes, to smoke and converse.

Over port wine, Toad proved circumspect. He stood feet wide apart, back straight, proud and respectful before a portrait painted in oils of his

"Searching for something important overlooked – a useful clue"

great-ancestor, Sir. Hugh Mungas Toad, hung above the spacious fireplace. About to address his guests to the obvious failures in the justice system, of the fashionably lax attitude toward serious offences, particularly, along by the riverbank, when occurred a noise outside – a powerful motor screeching up. Quickly, everybody's attention diverted to the driveway. An elderly butler scurried in, bowing and saying in a low voice to his master, "'E's coom, sir, young Mr Fox at the door."

"Dandy," exclaimed Toad, beside himself with glee, gesturing with his paw. "Show 'im in, show 'im in, simply adore the fella. Bit of a lady's man – show off, wot, and, by gad, quick at the wheel, a real motor racer."

Badger cringed, the mention of fast cars brought

on hideous memories of Toad's numerous traffic offences and his eventual painful incarceration before penitence and reform held sway.

A nimble, bushy-tailed fox entered the precincts of the lamplit library.

The chums sat in leather club chairs smoking, the fox presented a dashing athletic presence, full of charm and bonhomie.

"Dandy, me boy, so nice to see you again." In his exuberance, Toad sprang on his ham thighs from the corner, plonking down to greet the impeccably smart dresser, turned out in a reddish motoring cape, country tweeds by Jeeves & Hawkes, lilac spats, a foppish cap placed rakishly at an angle. "Clever as you are," Toad gushed, hopping up and down. "The sheer gall, the madness – just for a bet outwitted how many hunts is it now? The Malvern, the Chester, the Lextonby – by Gad, running against a pack. Those hounds are in tip-top condition, raring to rip you apart – maul you to death. That requires a deal of nerve, don't you agree you lot?" Toad guffawed.

Old Badger merely raised his glass, feeling somewhat ill-at-ease. "Money to be made out of bets, certainly. Me, I'm not a betting man."

"Your loss," answered the fox, plucking a Turkish gasper from his silver cigarette case.

"Glass of whisky suit yer, old bean." Mr Toad grabbed the decanter twinkling by the firelight, pouring a large measure.

"Don't mind if I do." The fox smirked, then caught sight of Mr Beaver's cynical expression. He sensed an obtuse snub.

Meanwhile, lost in admiration for this reckless daredevil, so like himself in many ways, who always managed to live to fight another day, although Toad might have been starstruck, his friends remained notably unimpressed.

"Bloodsports," murmured Badger, putting a damper on proceedings, savouring his rolled-leaf cigar. "Not so keen on 'em myself."

"Me and Toady prefer to live in the fast lane," emphasised red fox with a wink, flourishing his cigarette. "How are yer, Mr Beaver? You a stay-at-home sort of chappie? Dams and water features your tune, ain't it?"

"Tracking down a murder, actually," replied the large marine rodent forcefully. Black triangular ears twitched, the fox's bright eyes became wary. He tried to swiftly change the subject.

"Fella bet a fortune on my demise t'other day – Medbury Hunt, I think it was, Sir Harry Balfour's turnout."

"To continue," cut in Beaver. "Nine ducks were killed night before last, mutilated in a most heinous manner, their families left to grieve, to deal with the appalling aftermath. Funny how employing my trusty magnifying lens, so derided by the official rural police force round here, I've managed to retrieve a startling piece of evidence crucially missed by the inspector."

The fox merely sneered.

"I've read in the papers about your silly magnifying lens antics. What was it, 'robbery at

Toad Hall', or some such drivel. *What evidence?*"

"Such a dreadful pity, dandy," said Beaver caustically. "Your mislaying that platinum diamond cufflink, losing it like that, I mean."

"LIKE WHAT?"

"Distinctively shaped, lucky horseshoe, isn't it? Now, to my eye, my observation at least, that appears to match that swanky tie pin you're wearing. What bad luck, I found your errant cufflink in amongst the carnage of the duck hatchery. The complete set sold exclusively by *John Aspinals* of Bond Street, est 1778. The police will check the books, of course. Arrest this scoundrel," Beaver bellowed contemptuously. "Showing off to your vixen girlfriend, needing little encouragement, I'd say. Blood lust at its most debased."

Beside himself with rage, the red fox, understanding the full gravity of these allegations and where they shall ultimately lead, retrieved a handgun from his pocket and sprang forward to aim the muzzle directly at Mr Beaver's temple, ready enough to pull the trigger and blow his brains out. Thereafter, an odd circumstance intruded upon the scene. Perhaps encouraged by the evil of the situation, an old foe materialised, recognisable by that strangely undulating broad brow, the calculating, somewhat amused expression. Was it Professor James Moriarty, or Dandy Fox pressing the service revolver to his head. How many moments of existence remaining?

"Mr Holmes, Mr Holmes," an audibly human voice registered, a cup and saucer on a tray rattled.

Dimly, the retiree gathered his wits about him. The calming presence of his domestic came into focus leaning over the settee. The pleasing surroundings of the Downland cottage materialised. Order was promptly restored by a much needed pot of Brazilian coffee. The Kenneth Graham book was on the floor where it had fallen off his lap. Mrs Cobbs picked it up.

"Please, Mrs Cobbs," said he, his left hand trembling. "Remove that tin of Saphir Médaille d'Or at once. Throw it away. The dustbin, anywhere."

Holmes, although feeling more his old self, inwardly cursed his weak nature, resolving in future to bear reform, keep strictly to his mellower tobacco regime – Ogden's Cobnut Sliced – without resort to the fumy realms of immature fantasy engulfing his mind. Anyhow, friend Watson should not approve of this temporary lapse that reminded the retired consulting detective he was due to play a round of golf at Crowbury links on Saturday, which cheered him up no end.

Platform Vandal

Findon branch line station was built in the country house, timber-cladded style with a tile-hung upper storey and incised plasterwork. Spanning the up and down lines, between platforms, an elaborate ironwork footbridge.

Due to the weather, a long delay had left old Mr Holmes both frozen and infuriated. The waiting room was closed to passengers, a wretched inconvenience for one normally expected, in mid-December, a nice banked-up coal fire in the grate, a good blaze going – but not today. One of the porters was up a stepladder assessing a broken waiting room window, evidence of vandalism.

"I'se tells Sergeant Clarke, I wont's this blighter

caught – young or old. Somebody las' night deliberately broke the station windas. Chucked rocks, thas serious, railway property, see."

"Drunken louts from the ale houses," offered Holmes disinterestedly, tying the flaps of the deerstalker more firmly over his ears. "'The Anchor' and 'The Station Hotel' attract their fair share of riff-raff, do they not?"

"Mebbe. The sergeant tol' me 'e thinks it were done in the early hours, no one about. My, if I could jest gets me mits on tha's sods. Pardon me," the porter apologised, climbing down the steps. "Me, I'd 'ave 'em up afore the justice, I would."

"Although, you have no idea who was responsible."

"Mebbe, ol' Tom Stavey, the village idiot 'e's pals

goadin' 'im on. 'E be big an' daft enough, alrigh', for a dare, like."

Thereafter, a pause in conversation took place due to the din as a heavy goods rattled through.

"Mr Smith," asked Holmes, gritting his teeth against the perishing cold, "I had best make my way over the footbridge to catch my train. Exactly when is it due?" He cast a withering gaze along to the bleak platform's end. What with snow delays, 'a hundred years', he half expected the porter to say.

"'Bout seven minutes 'fore the train is due. I'll jest clip your ticket, sir."

Mr Eades, the bearded stationmaster, made an appearance leaning round the door to his office, smoking his pipe. Despite a cravat, the piercing cold cut into Holmes' neck, his angular cheek bones, and his nose was running. Over the way was a goods siding, at the end of which resided a red-brick loco shed just big enough to stable a single engine – roof tiles patchy white. Further up the line was the gated level crossing, a twenty- two-leaver framed signal box dating from 1876, smoke rising from a little chimney. A separate hut provided for lamps and oil. Supervising sacks being loaded onto a cart was the coal merchant Mr Phelps. The morning remained wintry and overcast with occasional spells of weak sunshine, snow flurries gusting up the platform – definitely not the place to be stood doing nothing. The vacuum of stillness was palpable, as though the station was holding its breath – incredulous that the next train would really arrive.

Regardless of the curious gaze of a bystander

coming down the steps from the footbridge – a plump, bespectacled chap wearing a sheepskin coat and tweed cap – a second passenger hardy enough to endure the bitter wind currently blowing along the tracks. For want of nothing better to do, Holmes chose to amble across to the fence on which were displayed printed tin adverts for *Wright's Coal Tar Soap'* and 'Lipton's Tea'. A waste bin beckoned, or rather the discarded red scarf curled up amongst the usual litter. A cursory examination revealed the fabric overstretched – a dusty white deposit adhering to the cloth. The slight scent of lavender water indicated a lady's accoutrement.

Holmes flung the scarf back amongst the rubbish, proceeding to stroll meditatively up towards the platform's end. Further along was the porter's garden plot, his flower bed in summer alive with colourful geranium blooms, but at present just rows of canes poking up. The name F – DON STATION spelled in whitewashed stones, two of these stones notable by their absence. Clear indentations visible amongst the clods of earth. So, the stones had been recently forcibly removed. The only other possible clue to criminal intent was a tiny brass key trodden into the crinkled ice formed along the platform's edge.

"Elementary," said the retiree out loud, pleased his eyesight was still up to the mark, his acute observation unimpaired.

"Eh, what's that?" enquired the fellow, frowning.

"Oh nothing, pardon me. I was just talking to myself." Holmes laughed it off. "My advanced years, y'know."

A train puffed in, there were few passengers on board.

"I must say," said the beetroot-faced fellow, prattling on, grateful to be comfortably seated in a corner of a warm compartment they had to themselves. "Mr Smith's really got his hands full, not only will those windows require putty and re-glazing, but I suppose the railway people may never find the culprit."

"I think I already know the culprit," answered elderly Mr Holmes blithely.

The chap's jaw dropped in surprise. "You actually know who broke the station windows – village idiot Staveley gets my vote."

"I don't judge it was he. Alright, I understand

he's a bit dim up top, but that type often get the blame."

"Then, I beseech you, for heaven's sake, my dear sir, tell me who you suspect of being the window smasher. Please, I beg you."

"'Fraid not." Holmes was emphatic, also quietly satisfied.

The fat chap, somewhat huffily, unfolded his copy of the *Times*, proceeding with the crossword.

Holmes wondered which was the best way forwards. He decided on the direct approach.

Just off the High Street, the cheerful lights of the shops, and inns aglow, snow pattering down, led Holmes to the porch of postman's cottage. A brief rap at the door knocker, the horn lantern resplendent on its hook, a squat, dumpy woman –

all smiles – answered the summons.

"Mrs Thurlston, may I return this. I recall you wearing a similar at the Christmas fayre held at the village hall last week. In a trifling better condition, of course." He bowed slightly.

Mrs Thurlston was no doubt charmed by this tall, spritely, eighty-year-old offering the bright red fabric for her appraisal.

"Not mine," she barely gave it a glance. "Coming in for a sherry? Sorry, I haven't anything stronger. Did you manage to arrange for Mr Foley to do the bookstall for our next jumble?"

"I did, Margery, can I touch you for one of your Du Maurier cigarettes?

"Course you can. That's it, take a pew by the fire. How's your golfing partner, Watson, bearing up?

After Christmas nothing to do but hibernate at this time of season is there!"

Thus, the fireside conversation between the jumble committee members passed pleasantly. Pleasantly enough, that is, until Holmes was about to leave, prepared to make the trudge up the Downland footpath from the village to his cottage.

"Bye the bye," mentioned he on the doorstep, pulling up his coat collar against the snow blowing off the Downs, "you mustn't act so rashly in future. I know from personal experience Smith can be annoying, a stickler for rules and regulations."

"The porter? What do I care for Smith?"

"My dear Mrs Thurlston, evidently a great deal. Enough to cross the footbridge and, using your scarf as a sling, hurl a number of whitewashed stones garnered from the platform flowerbed, breaking the glass of a number of windows, meaning I and other passengers suffered the ravages of exposure. All because, I'd wager, earlier the previous day you found yourself at the station accused of travelling without a valid ticket. Thus, you were clobbered by Mr Smith for excess fair. Your ticket, no doubt, innocently mislaid."

"What rot you speak," said she hotly. "Of course, Mr. Holmes, I've read about your Baker Street associations, but really."

"Furthermore, Mr Smith was only doing his job. Later that night, I propose unable to accept having to pay for another ticket, seething with pique, you, Mrs Thurlston, returned to the station resorting to vandalism. Bye the bye, I return this little brass

"Mrs Thurlston, returned to the station resorting to vandalism"

key – fits that most excellent novelty Christmas matchbox of yours from which I lit my cigarette. Inside one compartment contains a wind-up mechanism, the other a miniature Christmas tree seen from above, circled by carol singers that goes round and round. Quite charming. Goodnight to you."

Pebblesea Lighthouse

For a bracing walk, in close contact with the sea, elderly Mr. Holmes liked nothing better than to follow the path alongside the chalk cliffs from Seabury Head to Pebblesea Lighthouse.

An altogether brisk trudge where one met hardly another soul. Save plenty of bob tailed rabbits for the dog to chase, else colonies of nesting gulls inhabiting the cliffs.

Out to sea, at the height of summer, fisher boats skirted round the coast in tranquil, sparkling blue waters.

The dog bounded ahead when approaching Berwick Gap, a fair-haired girl of about sixteen, wearing a white smock and bonnet caught Holme's attention.

She was knelt perilously close to the cliff edge, pummelling the overhanging grass tufts with balled fists.

"Oh, wont someone help!" she wailed.

Were God forbid Holmes and his pooch about to witness a young impetuous maiden fling herself onto the rocks?

Thus, the elderly man prepared to remonstrate with the girl. Offer good fellowship although this proved unnecessary. For at that moment a clamour of barking broke out.

Upon realizing she was spotted, the dog being brought to heel, the young lady jumped up, running off in the direction of Pebblesea Church.

Taking a deep breath, Mr. Holmes put this

childish tantrum episode out of his mind, making due haste along the rough track.

The day was boiling hot, the sun at its zenith, glaring from a cloudless sky.

Fortunately, one of the few habitations along this stretch of the coastline came into view. Alas Holmes forgetting to pack his water flask in his knapsack had grown very thirsty, his throat felt parched.

The coastguard's wife would not begrudge him a cup of water surely, and a bowl for the dog.

Folk in this region of the lighthouse, situated up on the cliff were no doubt used to walkers and holiday sightseers.

However, the solidly built coastguard's cottage overseeing the glistening waters of the channel seemed to him deserted. Yet Holmes' thirst persisted. He was going to have a drink of water, come what may.

Perchance maybe there was an outside tap round the back.

"Hey Ho!" called a voice.

He turned to find a matronly woman, with a wrinkly brown face beckoning from the stone porch, "local, is we?"

"Findon way," he strode towards her grinning, "I wonder if I could beg a drink of water?"

"I be Mrs. Nutson, the housekeeper," said she formally, "The Coastguard, Mr. Firle and e's wife be gone to see the vicar. Back in an hour 'spect… what a soppy dog you have. Here dearie Oi'll fetcha' bowl, come on in Sir, grab a bit o' shade. Oi'll put the kettle on. The cold tap is along the way, rinse yer face why don't yer".

"I shall absolutely take advantage of your sink madam, thank you".

"Yer welcome." she replied.

Whilst Mrs. Nutson managed the hob and kettle, Holmes stooped along a low-ceilinged passageway, minding, not to hit his head but alas not his business. Curse his enquiring mind, for he had spied a partly opened door on his left.

Nudging it open further, he became aware of a dark and gloomy shuttered room, pungent with the scent of lilies. His eyes taking time to adjust after the suns glare, he understood mirrors to be draped in black, light from a solitary candle revealing, central to the pinewood floor, an open coffin lined with taffeta, supported on trestles.

This encouraged a pang of horror, for the old fellow quickly realised the coffined occupant seemed dreadfully familiar.

The same snub nose and dimpled mouth, the pronounced cleft chin. Why, this deceased girl's face was in every aspect the exact likeness of the young lady he saw earlier knelt at the cliff edge. Save for a thick bandage swaddling her head.

A fatal injury to the cranium he deduced.

Gently closing the door, he went to dab his face and neck from the tap. Proceeding thence back to the cottage parlour, now much intrigued.

"I'm so sorry Mrs. Nutson, I couldn't help noticing…"

The woman understood instantly. "Lor', I shoulda' shut thar door. It's a pity so it be. The

Coastguards daughter, Mary Firle. Whoy, the poor darlin'll get a noice fooneral, buried in the ole graveyard over at Pebblesea Church."

"The coastguard's daughter you say!"

The old housekeepers' eyes glistened with unmistakeable sorrow. "Aye, a tragic accident, Mary fell to her death. Evenin' afore last. Oi reckons that sea fog be to blame. Lost her footing. The coast path can be hard to follow when them fogs close in."

Holmes agreed, "The fogs are a wretched bind. I and my friend Watson often play golf at Seabury head links. In a matter of a very short while fog wafts in, the coast becomes engulfed, the game is abandoned and it's back to the clubhouse – My sympathy's."

Old Mr. Holmes accepted a mug of tea. "I do not

wish to burden you further Mrs. Nutson, but on my walk earlier I encountered a young lady on the cliff whose face was an exact likeness of your employer's late daughter. The resemblance was striking. She is related I presume?"

The old woman lit her short clay pipe and nodded, "That'd be Lorna her twin, wandering the cliffs moping, coming to terms, as we all must. She b'aint be daft mind sir. Just desperate to bring her sister back. Which she wont, ever – no amount o' staring out to sea awt' otherwise!"

"I saw her on the cliff at Berwick Gap."

"That'll be where Mary fell. Cruel fate, the sea fog. Wh' cannus mortal folks do against tha'?"

The elderly retiree heard a somewhat cynical inner voice murmur *'fell? Or was she pushed?'*

Smoking her pipe, the house servant was drawn to study the retiree's absorbed expression, the way his brow furrowed. "Be ye aroit Sir?"

"Perfectly," he answered curtly, "I trust the funeral shall be well attended Mrs. Nutson. Please pass on my condolences to the Coastguard Mr. Firle and his wife. Good day."

———

At Pebblesea Lighthouse, one notable landmark perched at the summit of the green slope of Downs, Holmes smartly turned round, dog and man descending back down the way they had come.

They halted at Berwick Gap to enjoy the sun and view, until, on a whim he decided to examine the immediate area of cliff top where he had earlier encountered Lorna beating her fists.

The dog gave himself a little shake, happy enough to shuffle amongst the furze.

Brandishing his ash stick, Holmes advanced along the cliff edge, peering at the waves crashing against the wooden groins, the rocks foamy with meandering sea spray. Those same fateful rocks, where Lorna's twin lost her life.

He made a close search of the immediate vicinity. Observing how the bright white stones used to mark out the coast path on one side, that is the side closest to the cliffs edge, appeared to have been tampered with, recently lifted, leaving a noticeable imprint. He also deduced, hurriedly replaced, not quite to true. A small sized stone inhabiting a larger one's nook.

The retiree was seriously concerned. The dog padded over.

He began to talk out loud. Making communion with man's best friend – Banding theories about freely, to his four-legged Doctor Watson. "What if, old boy, supposing someone... a jealous fella, supplanted in Mary's affections by another. Knowing full well she would be on foot, walking back that way, hoped to meet that evening upon the cliff to confront her. But when the sea fog rolled in an awful opportunity for revenge presented itself. Frankly, to commit murder."

Cocking its head to one side, the dog gave Holmes its full and undivided attention.

"My supposition be this, what if a dastardly scheme is hatched, thus working free a number of white marker stones he makes the coast path deviate, leading the trusting traveller not safely along beside the cliff edge, but most assuredly over it!"

Barking like mad, the dog agreed, receiving a firm pat on the forehead for its trouble.

"A most credible subterfuge – enough to fool the Coastguard, the Police and locals, but most decidedly not, Sherlock Holmes. We must make haste to the Coastguard's cottage and enquire of the Firle's if they knew of any romantic tiffle concerning their late daughter Mary. Her killer must be brought to justice and face the rigours of the law."

Pausing to observe the last vestiges of a glorious sunset, the heat of the day much lessened, striding along the path, down into the dip old Mr. Holmes was alerted by a curious flicker of light farther afield than his current destination, the Coastguard's cottage.

Damnably queer this, for the unexpected source was none other than Pebblesea Lighthouse.

The landmark had to his knowledge been decommissioned, unused for many years. The great diamond paned reflector lamp shone no more.

The dog growing weary of his excursion couldn't care less. Wanting instead its dinner, its basket and to be fussed over by Mrs Cobbs.

A particular case from the Baker Street years came into Sherlock's mind. A different setting, but emotionally similar. The retired detective increased his stride, yelling to his Labrador not to slouch so, and to keep up.

Hastening past the coastguard's cottage, once more his attention was taken by that glimmer of light from the old disused lighthouse.

"Too late, too late", he muttered. Realising this solitary light most surely caused by a candle left to burn. The feeble flame greatly magnified by the myriad glass panels of the reflector.

Facts began to reassert themselves.

How came the crux of this sorry business? If Holmes' theory proved correct – there must needs be a second fatal consequence.

Approaching the door to the decommissioned lighthouse, the old fellow observed the padlock. His dog started whining. The rusty chains hung loose.

Holmes's breath quickened, for he surmised whoever mounted up those twisty steps, did so to take one last look from the lamp room, at the sunset over the channel. A lit candle in memory of what could have been.

Poor, foolish youth. A final hopeless gesture born of inconsolable grief upon the eve of his victim's funeral.

The method of despatch in such cases – poison, a shotgun, maybe the use of a razor drawn swiftly across the throat, or a rope to hang oneself by.

No sooner through the door, it was found plainly a stout rope, a very long one was responsible for an almost instantaneous deliverance.

The bovine, thick lipped boy with tussled hair, his neck very broken, face tinted a bluey purple, had decided to fling himself from the top step. To drop into a dark well of oblivion. The neck, thick as a

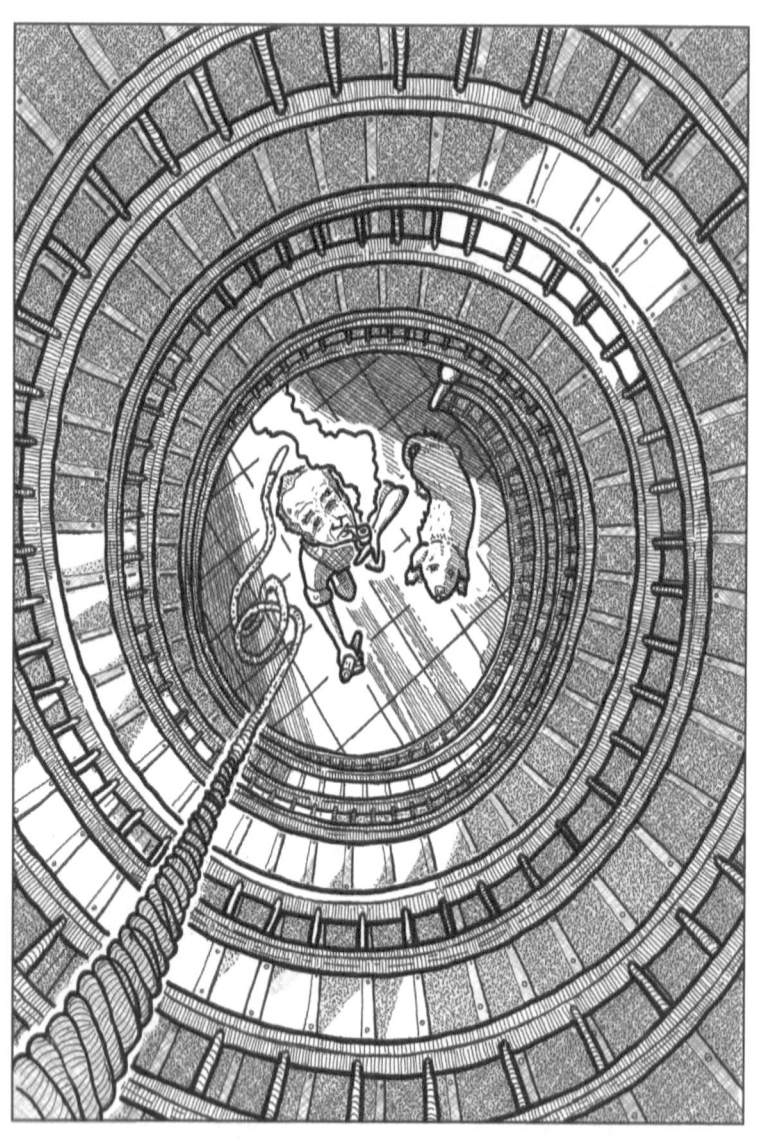

"It was found plainly a stout rope"

bull's, snapped by the velocity of the fall.

Attired in corduroy trousers, neckerchief, rough shirt, and hob-nailed boots, the penitent swung like a heavy pendulum, his time done, a final act, being the mandatory note of confession poking from the top pocket of his moleskin waistcoat.

Mr. Falcon Smith

Resident of Findon, Falcon Smith, penned crime novels for a living *The Hat Rack Hanging* and *The Cottage Strangler* amongst his most popular titles, available at many libraries and bookshops.

Although like Holmes, getting on a bit, he was a sprightly seventy five years young and had only started writing in his late fifties, not many locals had the faintest notion that the elderly golfer who lived in a very nice house at the base of the downs was, in fact, a professional author by trade.

One morning, Falcon Smith, ensconsed in his study, seemed terribly distracted, staring out of the latticed window at the sunny lawn, supposedly on the pretence of allowing a plot to form in his mind.

Abruptly, he thumped the blotter with his fist, declaring loudly to himself, "I must get him, perhaps he may be able to sort out this puzzle – Mrs. Dumpole!" He called out to his domestic.

The servant woman came hurrying into his study, wiping gleaming red hands on her apron.

"Sherlock Holmes, the retired consulting detective, you know where he lives?" he asked.

"Old Horseshoe Cottage Sir, up on the downs!" she answered, "do you want me to take a message – I'm going that way with the dog."

"Yes, yes, I think you might Mrs. Dumpole. Be so good as to wait for a minute. I shall just jot down a note now."

The woman did as bidden. So thus, it was old Mr. Holmes was quietly reading a newspaper on his sofa before luncheon, when he received an urgent request for his services.

Mrs. Cobbs cooed from the kitchen range, "Ooh, Falcon Smith, I did so like his last one Mr. Holmes, did you read it? *The Hat Rack Hanging*, got it from the library last week. 'Mystery writer', isn't that the modern slang for such people?" she laid out knives and forks on the starched linen.

Why, that fellow seen briefly at the clubhouse bar, distantly on the links. Holmes had indeed read a couple of his books, so lost no time studying the message. Mrs. Dumpole still nattering on the porch step outside. Glad for the warmth emanating from the crackling coals, the Labrador stretched himself on the hearth rug.

Dear Holmes,

I am in desperate need of your abilities. Call on me this evening if you can. An impossible mystery awaits.

Sincerely yours
Falcon Smith

"For your benefit Holmes, I shall elaborate upon certain *facts*," proposed the old literary trooper (emphasising the word facts), knowing full well the no nonsense reputation of his guest.

Crossing his legs Mr. Smith lit a cheroot, "My valuable silver plate is kept securely locked in a cabinet in the dining room. A glass fronted antique I purchased in Steyning some time ago. A burglar somehow got into my house and stole certain items from this same cabinet – that's a given. Now, you may or may not know this Holmes but I am a successfully published crime novelist and am quite knowledgeable on the burglar's mentality, because I used to work as a barrister. First at Lincolns Inn, then at Brighton in the criminal courts, dealing with this sort of thing, housebreaking and so forth. Dammit sir, I am like yourself, well acquainted with the rudiments of how a thief goes about breaking and entering a property. Country place, town villa, or otherwise. I make a very respectable living from thinking up new and original ways of doing just that, and yet Holmes, I cannot for the life of me fathom what actually occurred on Wednesday last. Upon a dark and windy afternoon, when I was entertaining a dear friend of mine – Mrs. Gladys Alcott."

Glancing up, the retired detective recognised the name instantly. "I quite like Alcott, lives over at Sumpting doesn't she?" said Holmes, putting down his pipe. "Her lady detective Peggy Derwent is very convincing, like Catherine Perkis's Loveday Brookes, for arsenic you can't beat her. Those jolly awful vicars and dashing young cads out to poison female relations with pots of money. Aunts simply drop like flies – *Derwent Gets Her Man* and *Derwent and the Cotswold Killer* spring to mind."

"Quite", Falcon Smith stubbed out his half-smoked cheroot. "But to continue, Mrs. Alcott and I were chatting about our shared passion for Gilbert and Sullivan. Both of us partaking of hot buttered crumpets, a first-rate tea spread before us, Mrs. Dumpole I must emphasise busy in the kitchen scrubbing vegetables. During our tête-à-tete Gladys, that is Mrs. Alcott, announced she had brought with her a signed copy of her latest book, no surprises there. She then manoeuvred her wheeled chair closer to where I was sat in this same armchair – also keen to show me a delightful gold locket, that her husband Crispen had purchased from Bond Street on account of their wedding anniversary." He paused, then continued, "The clock on the mantlepiece said ten to three. I remember that particularly, next I knew the chimes of three o' clock suddenly rang out. I was left confused, time, where had it gone? When last, I recall commenting on Mrs. Alcotts locket, thanking her for the book yet ten whole minutes had passed which I couldn't account for. Gladys appeared not to have noticed anything untoward about my demeanour. Thus, things proceeded as ordinarily as they will. Our tea concluded, Martin her chauffeur pushed her wheelchair back to the car. They drove off to Sumpting shortly after."

"You have not I trust, been under pressure of work lately, working too hard? You authors are quite obsessive after all."

"No more than usual," he replied thoughtfully. "Anyhow, I had barely settled down again when piercing screams came from the dining room. My heart sank as poor Mrs. Dumpole, halfway hysterical with worry came tearing in here babbling that certain of my silverware was missing. The top shelf of the *still locked* cabinet bereft of a valuable antique silver engraved 17th century dish, and a silver casket which I swear to you was present and correct when my domestic and I visited the dining room earlier that day to position a flower vase. She led me straight away to a window part open, the latch drawn back, the dining room curtains blowing in the breeze." He paused, "Well Mr. Holmes, aint you about to snatch up that famous magnifying glass and head straight outside to frantically search the flower bed beneath the windowsill for footprints. I confess, I certainly did and found absolutely nothing. Now, didn't you suspect the chauffeur, Martin? That's just too simplistic, he's a splendid fellow whose been in Glady's employ for many years."

"That did cross my mind yes. But the facts just don't add up. A typical break in, no I think not. You were wise to alert me to mischief. This crime it appears, demands careful analysis".

"I trust we may dismiss any suggestion that I myself contrived to… erm."

"We can," answered Holmes tersely, "I have already formed my own worthy hypothesis. Let us retrace our steps… We return again to that Wednesday afternoon. The authoress of Peggy Derwent novels is comfortably situated in her wheeled chair, close by yourself, the true infamy of this crime is about to unfold. The crime writer, famous for her villainous books herself takes on the role of villain"

"Villain! I say I'm not having that. Won't have a

word said against her." he stammered in vehement protest.

"Well Smith, you are about to hear a good deal of words said against her for I shall presently outline the method. I'd listen very carefully if I were you, for the sake of future relations".

He steepled his long bony fingers together, an old habit from the Baker Street years.

Logs in the grate crackled, whilst outside gusts of rain swept across the lawn, for it was a breezy day.

"To put it bluntly Smith, you were in my view undoubtedly the victim of *hypnosis* – I propose Mrs. Alcott whisked the locket in front of your face, waving it as a pendulum, in a trice your mind should be subdued to her will to do her bidding. It was I fear you alone, or rather your subconscious

"He steepled his long bony fingers together"

that obeyed her instructions, removing the cabinet key from your desk. Thereafter in a trance going directly to the dining room and opening the cabinet door. Quite naively removing the valuable items," a thin smile appeared upon his lips. "It's all a simple matter of submitting your will to hers Smith, why man, your actions should have been second nature. You must have shown off your silver to her on many occasions."

"Hypnotised." The author exclaimed, "What an idea for a plot. Confound it, snapping her fingers **JUST AS THE CLOCK STRIKES THREE**, yes! I'm with you Holmes."

"One can but conjecture Mrs. Alcott's husband Crispin has links with London's magic circle, stage producer, impresario, isn't he? She undoubtedly

Mrs. Dumpole

learnt her accomplishments as a hypnotist from say, a member of the circle. You'd better put a good face on it when next you ask for the prompt return of the items – you can also explain how she did it." concluded Holmes.

"By Jove, I think I'll do just that Holmes. I suppose her next book will be based on all this, what a nerve!"

"No doubt about it – a best seller I'm sure," laughed the elderly retiree, watching a flock of starling's land on the lawn.

The Lost Pudding

A light sprinkling of snow pattering the window, elderly Mr. Holmes, presently inhabiting the heated railway carriage of the Steyning bound service, hauled by a Terrier Tank engine, steaming through the Wealden landscape, refolded The Times newspaper.

Watson, good old Watson, he had been to visit his friend and golfing partner in Horsham.

Gazing out of the window, the train was about to enter a station. Southwater, known for its thriving brickworks, was soon left behind. Then at West Grinstead, a tall, very attractive blonde lady boarded the train and by way of conversation realising the identity of her illustrious fellow passenger went on to make an astounding assertion.

Removing her kid gloves, her face brightly aglow, rosy cheeked from waiting on the platform. The woman seemed genuine enough the more her talk unfolded, details shared.

"How fortuitous," she declared. "I recall your picture in the Findon times. You won the golf tournament at Crowbridge. Mr. Sherlock Holmes, isn't it? The consulting detective of Baker Street renown."

"If it pleases you, although I'm long retired now. I rarely visit London. But your reference to the golf is accurate."

"You know. It takes me back to when I was a girl at Roedean. I won for a school prize a set of your cases written by your esteemed biographer Dr.

Watson."

The lady's name was Felicity Long married with two daughters – Lumina Jane and Zita Marie. Her family only recently taken up residence in her late uncles substantial detached villa in Henfield. Having been beneficiaries of his generous will.

"I know this must sound absurd, but I put it to you – can a ghost be a thief? Is a ghost capable of stealing?"

Holmes found himself slow to answer such a preposterous question.

"If so," she frowned, "My late uncle no less, was responsible for pinching a Christmas pudding. Hilda my cook, screaming the house down actually witnessed his ghost. She came running upstairs to my room – when we ourselves returned to the kitchen and the pudding was gone."

"Unlikely, but charmingly seasonal. Nonetheless Mrs. Long - I am old and wise enough not to be entirely dismissive. Allow me to make a note in my pocketbook. Pray, what did your late uncle do in life anyhow?"

"Why Mr. Durbridge-Woolcombe was a committed antiquarian collector. I personally knew little of him until our solicitor informed us of our good fortune."

"I see." Holmes did a good job of concealing his sarcasm when he next spoke, "And your cook importantly claims to have actually sighted this house ghost, surely only one of a few living allowed such a privilege, psychical, mediumistic?"

"Pray, what did your late uncle do in life anyhow?

"I think not. Hilda is a straightforward, sane and cheerful northerner from Didbury in Manchester. We adore her. She is sweet tempered as a rule and fusses over us like an old hen."

"Describe her."

"Short, tubby, has thick legs, ties her hair back in a bun, in her sixties"

"That will do." Mr. Holmes was not exactly brim-full of ambitious solutions, nor quite sure how best to proceed: Partridge Green station, with its goods siding full of fertilizer wagons, came into view.

"You know," said the woman smiling sweetly. "I confess while we've been talking, I was seized by an idea. Is it just too selfish, too self-serving, too much to expect, that you being a local over at Findon, might expand your enquiries by visiting my house in Henfield with a view to solving this mystery. This coming Friday should suit – my husband will be working late in the city. To be really honest Mr. Holmes, I'd really like you to autograph my first edition copies of your books."

Old Mr. Holmes' normally icy reserve simply vapourised before Mrs. Longs obvious charm and sincerity, allowing himself to investigate surely the most ludicrous case of his career, "Friday you say, five o'clock do?" Before adding, "One further point. You and your family have only recently moved in. How pray was cook able to so surely identify the likeness of this ghost Durbridge Woolcombe?"

"The house we inherited in Henfield still contains much of my late relatives' furnishings and belongings, collected over a lifetime. There is a distinguished portrait in oils, gilt frames and glassed, that hangs above the fireplace in the sitting room. I grant you, by the look of him, a genial approachable fellow – The most unlikely of agitated spectres!"

———

Not far from Henfield station, the railway hotel nearby – a brisk walk along the road eventually leads past St. Peters church.

The retired consulting detective stopped at no.68, an attractive timber framed property 'The Laurels' rooved in mossy Horsham slates with fine brick chimneys. Mrs. Long and her daughters were there to greet him on the porch.

Over a pot of tea Hilda the cook could not have been more amiable and when gently questioned remained adamant she had actually seen a ghost – she would swear to it on the bible.

Felicity Long herself, insisted giving Holmes a

short tour of the house – showing him a fraction of the artifacts collected over her uncle's lifetime, filling every room.

"We shall have to sling most of it out," the lady proclaimed, "I and my girls have a large bonfire planned in the back garden to burn a good deal of papers, and so forth."

"Might it not be prudent to have the artifacts judged by an expert?" Mr. Holmes enquired seriously. "You may be pleasingly surprised and make some money. Greens emporium along the High Street will give you a valuation, I'm sure."

Patting her knees Mrs. Long merely laughed.

"Durbridge Woolcombe, that is what we know of him was a true gentleman eccentric, a committed antiquarian collector with more money than sense.

Guilty of filling this house from top to bottom with stacks of memorabilia and useless knick-knacks – and I love him the more for that. Although I do wish he wouldn't pester us as a ghost… Greens you say? Well, I will make enquiries."

"If I have anything to do with it Mrs. Long," remarked Holmes, eyeing the oil portrait above the fireplace. "Your spectral uncle shall be laid to rest fair and square, sooner rather than later."

On arrival Holmes recalled entering the sitting room seeing a comfortable sofa, beside this was placed a large dolls house. More accurately, children's playhouse guarded by a wooden hinged sausage dog on wheels. This set him to thinking.

"The playhouse for your daughters is both of generous proportions and well crafted," mentioned he, stooping down to peer through the paneless windows, admiring the little wooden Swiss style chairs and table.

"A Mr. Dunster at Pococks toy shop in Steyning sold us the playhouse. Lumina and Zita enjoy larking about inside."

"Mrs. Hannigan, the ghost materialised where exactly?"

"Oh sir, up on the staircase." The plump, jolly woman replied. Eager to be of any assistance.

"I shall not argue the point – might I be permitted to look upstairs in the attic, you have lately adopted as a lumber room you were telling me Mrs. Long."

"Absolutely, so much junk!"

"Just so," replied the old gentleman deep in thought. "I shall require no more than ten minutes.

Zita Marie, whilst Mrs. Hannigan, your sister Lumina and I attain the higher regions be a good girl and list the contents – Every item, both fixtures and fittings of your dolls house – cook, lead the way."

Old Mr. Holmes ascended several flights of stairs to the top of the house, passing the servants landing until upon reaching the attic, he gingerly entered the makeshift lumber room and, thence mindful of knocking his head against any low beams, devoted his energies to conducting a brisk search. Nimbly opening trunks, lifting dust sheets, particularly alerted by a piercing crack of glass as his left foot contacted a wooden box on the floor. He nudged the toe of his shoe once more against the object causing a rattling noise.

Presumably losing interest, Lumina ran off back

downstairs.

An expression of pure glee filled the retiree's wrinkly face. For he had struck upon the answer.

———

Now returned to the sitting room, Mr. Holmes was more than ready to reveal his findings.

"Prepare yourselves," said he good humouredly, "for I am about to enlighten you as to how the ghost came to be – and the festive pudding vanished."

The girls seemed at this point uneasy and fidgety. The old fellow was at this point direct and to the point.

"To understand this business, we must firstly apply the lantern slide principle – I shall explain," he took a sip of his tea. "Earlier, upstairs in the attic my shoe providentially struck the side of a teak container tightly packed with glass photographic plates. One of these emulsion plates cracked on impact. Previously, you will recall I removed a dust sheet revealing plain as day a box camera with brass lens, tripod attachments. Bottles labelled 'emulsifier', additionally - a loose file of correspondence headed *Henfield Photographic Society,* for assuredly your uncle Woolcombe in life chose as his hobby, photography - possessing his own dark room to develop pictures at leisure, being on occasions himself photographed for posterity by like-minded friends in this new science - you follow?"

"Oh indeed Mr. Holmes, I can vouch for this dark room you talk of, was situated down in the basement."

Mrs. Long looked elated, knowing the retired detective was onto something. Her daughters merely scowled; this news was not pleasing to them.

"Your girls' plywood playhouse provides revealing clues as to how a ghost was raised – please note if you will, when the sitting room door is left open, as it is now, see how the window of the little house lines up perfectly with the wall beside the staircase. The wall space you will comprehend is painted plain magnolia. Zeta… recite your list if you will."

"Two chairs,

One table,

Curtains,

One teddy,

One small lamp,

One glass paperweight – "

"– Stop there. Now, I shall reveal the method in its entirety. One day exploring the attic as children will, your inquisitive daughters Mrs. Long, happened upon a box of photographic plates. One plate in particular, of your late uncle, took their fancy and they removed it, and with what I can only describe as childish genius, proposed to make him come alive. By matting out the background, leaving the old gentleman existent. That evening, making sure certain gas mantles were turned low, your father being no doubt busy in the city, no one else save cook about - just prior to Mrs. Hannigan quitting the kitchen to take a cup of tea up to your mother they utilised the pebble glass and little lamp to shine an

"What I can only describe as childish genius"

image onto the far wall."

The esteemed guest was more amused than critical while he autographed Mrs. Long's books.

"Tis true ma – every word – but then we wanted to put the pud back, but silly Zita dropped it outside on the garden path and Benny the dog ate it." Spoke up Lumina resolutely, pleased her and her sister managed to fool most everyone... save old Mr. Holmes from Findon.

Sally Sudbury's Christmas Tree

"Well, I never did," chortled Mrs. Cobbs, bringing through a plate of freshly baked scones. Sally Sudbury, our neighbour – what a fuss over nothing, an old, withered Christmas Tree still in its pot, she's been wanting to replant in the garden, gone missing from the back patio. I ask you; one would normally be grateful to get rid of such things – good luck to whoever stole it – for kindling to build a fire I'd guess."

Studying the obituary's old Holmes glanced up from the newspaper. "A splendid supposition."

"Really sir, well I'd say a man of the road certainly – January being so fearfully cold."

Folding his copy of The Times the retiree commented, "Sally Sudbury's dratted tree, which should probably have not rooted anyhow will be reduced to ash somewhere in a wooded dell. The evidence gone up in smoke. I mean when Sally visited earlier, I imagined she had mislaid her purse, or keys, something important."

"I don't know what you must think Mr. Holmes, now in your eightieth year being asked to investigate the loss of a worn-out tree. A dustman surely is the best person to consult. Anyway, what about the wretched pine needles, they will drop everywhere?"

Despite Mrs. Cobb's reservations, although finding his neighbour Mrs. Sudbury on occasions exasperating, Holmes fondly remembered '*The Case of the One-Legged Seagull'*, and for want of nothing better, putting on his coat and deerstalker, hurried across to her cottage, taking the flagged path to the porch with his dog.

Wearing her prim pinny and slippers, despite being busy at the Aga basting a joint, Sally was still insistant someone better had be brought to book for stealing her property.

Methodical as always, the retiree, long resident of the South Downs stepped out into the garden, shown by Sally the exact spot on the patio where the potted tree had stood awaiting replanting. His quick eyes lost nothing, following the mossy steps down, he took out his magnifying lens, gave a cursory examination of the greenhouse, which in summer was notable for its profusion of yellow and red tomato plants.

No prints on the doorknob, a lot of dead, dried out insects along a window ledge, cracked dingy panes of glass, again absent of smudges or useful finger marks. Wood panels in need of a good coat of paint though come spring. Thus, the greenhouse faded into mental obscurity, unable to hold his interest.

However, the clay brick wall beyond the leafy oblong of lawn with its prominent bird table showed distinct promise. Fruit saplings were at one time supported by wires, knocked into the brickwork by rusty nails. A piece of moleskin cloth had snagged, a cheeky robin redbreast in attendance, he focused upon his trusty lens, thus under magnification easily making out a seam with four stitch holes. Strands of navy-blue thread attached the material most likely ripped from a coat when a person clambered over into Mrs. Sudbury's garden.

His dog barked. Stood on tip toe the retired detective could make out the distant tiled roof, chimneys, lightning rod and weathervane atop of a rambling half-timber farmhouse across the downs.

He recalled how one day he had been out collecting for the church roof fund, only to be rebuffed by an unsavoury personality, told to clear off by one Philson Fennes, the owner of said property, whose grubby features, the shabby state of his clothes made him resemble a paupers revenant risen from the plague pit.

He was possessed of long uncut nails, more akin to talons and matted hair falling to his shoulders.

His beard clotted with food slops. In reality,

"A cheeky robin redbreast in attendance"

although of a miserly unkempt disposition, Fennes was worth a fortune from his late father's mills.

The potted fir tree now presented an intriguing conundrum. The pot itself surely a means of concealment. The close proximity of the millionaire Fennes' house begged the question – had something been stolen from there.

Leaving aside thoughts of the reclusive skinflint – elderly Mr. Holmes returned to Sally Sudbury's cottage.

Sat down in the opposite chimney piece, nursing a proffered mug of milky coffee, he asked if she might recognise the piece of moleskin cloth. Did it perchance belong to anyone she knew.

"No." Sally replied. She had no idea.

Thus, a scrap of material, a bit of blue thread an

old, vanished potted Christmas tree were all he had to go on.

A few months later, the matter all but forgotten, the retiree was out and about Findon on his bicycle, whence peddling round the corner of Plough Lane, journeying to post a letter, his memory was reignited regarding Mrs. Sudbury's lost tree.

In one of the cottage gardens, observed was a medium sized fir tree, planted crookedly. Parts of its root mass clawing up from the lumpy clods of earth of a vegetable patch. The garden belonged to a very pretty, recently restored cottage. A lucky horseshoe nailed to the front door.

A young fellow spun his petite wife round by the

washing line.

"Oh 'Enry do stop it! At once I say," chortled the lass playfully.

Hearing the gate clang, watching the retiree push his bike up the path. Henry Hartley, a familiar face in Findon for he worked at the greengrocers, known for his chirpy manner, beckoned the old man over to the washing line.

"Hello Mr. Holmes, oh I know your Mrs. Cobbs alrigh' – comes into the shop for veggies n' fruit, speaks after yer… 'Ere Mabel, lend a hand will yer' whitewashin' the cottage. Grab a brush dearie, get up the ladder sharpish or you'll be for it!" he called out merrily, full of beans, the sweethearts enjoying life to the full.

"No ta", she replied primly, going back indoors,

pausing to stroke her ginger cat.

"Well Henry," said Holmes, leaning on his bike, feeling the warmth of the sun on his face. "It seems like only yesterday this place was awfully run down. I recall how neglected it looked – what a splendid job you did eh."

"That's nice of you to say so Mr. Holmes, lots of hard graft. But me and my little ducky Mabel since we moved in, have done a lot. We're getting there."

"And to think Mr. Philsen Fennes who lives in that shuttered manor on the Downs and hardly sees daylight is helping fund your enterprise – hats off to both of you I say."

"Pardon me sir – did I hear correct. I can assure you no impropriety ever…"

"Enough," Holmes wagged his finger. "Spare me

your honest rhetoric, to think Sally Sudbury's Christmas tree that she meant to replant in her own garden is, by amazing coincidence rooted in your vegetable patch over there."

The lad was, at first, unable to respond, his face turning pale.

"But tell me truthfully Henry, what exactly were you up to in Mrs. Sudbury's Garden that cold early morning in January. I observe you are wearing for your whitewash endeavours a tatty three-quarter length moleskin coat, streaked with limewash and splatterings of green gloss paint. One of the seams is ripped, the piece of cloth I have at home shall fit it exactly. Perhaps your charming wife may stitch it back on... come Hartley I detest the man – tell me the truth – between us fellows, I'd be keen to know how exactly you broke into the manor. How did it all come about? I promise you our conversation shall remain confidential; you have my word."

"Alrigh', I'se give it to you straight sir... During Christmas week at the greengrocers, I gets asked by the governor to deliver two Christmas trees from our stock. One goes to a Mrs.Ridd up on The Downs, the other I takes for Sally Sudbury. Trotting along on the horse van after stopping off at Mrs. Ridd, I approached that ole' ramshackle farmhouse belonging to Mr. Fennes and this got me to finkin' – I'd heard he was a very wealthy, stay at home sort – common knowledge, despite having pots of money, e' rarely washed and looked like a bloomin' dosser. No servants either, lived on his own."

"I know, I've seen him," remarked the retiree,

quite unable to conceal his disgust. "The fellow possesses long yellowed fingernails, that resemble grotesque talons, pray continue."

"Well, Mr. Holmes - I thinks serious like – why should 'e have all the money an' me recently wed' always smartly turned out, in me shirt and tie, neatly pressed brown work-coat and polished boots, taking such care of my appearance. Why should I be hard up, putting every penny of me savings into me marriage. Including buying this run down, dilapidated cottage. See Sir, on my wages I could barely afford a dab of fresh paint, let alone sticks of furniture 'n Knick knacks my little duck has set her heart on from the department store in Worthing. Well, sat on the box seat of that delivery van, I got a chance to think big, and being the impetuous fool I am, pulled up by the verge, fed the horse his nosebag. Slipping into the overgrown garden I made me way to the back of the house. Five minutes later I had broken in through a rotten window, the catch loose and useless. Being dilapidated, the place had its advantages see. Philson Fennes sat in his long johns dozing in an armchair, all about heaps of empty bottles. I crept upstairs, amongst the damp, peeling wallpaper and cobwebs I located his bedroom and in that magnificent hovel, imagine my delight when I discovered beneath the mattress a roll of banknotes. A full fifty quid's worth kept in a sealed jam jar. Only a fraction of his hoarded wealth mind - but I 'aint stupid. What if Fennes reported the robbery to the police? I needed to conceal the loot somewhere else. Not at our place in Findon. Stolen

"A full fifty quid's worth kept in a sealed jam jar"

cash found on my property in person meant a long stretch in Lewes prison, losing my career prospects. That late afternoon, my next delivery took me to Sally Sudbury's cottage. The old dame asked me specific to help pot her festive tree for she was determined to replant it after Christmas."

"I recall she went indoors to make us a pot of tea and in that time, I realised a safe hiding place was close to hand. See, I managed to bury the jar deep in the soil and there the stolen money remained, part of that lady's Christmas without her even realising. Fennes never did report the burglary and come January I returned to 'claim what was mine'… sort of!"

The Worth Valley Mystery

The last week in March saw Mr. Holmes taking up a long-standing invitation to visit Dr. Watson's old nursing orderly Stamford, who had retired as a senior staff nurse at St. Bartholomew's teaching hospital, now living in a charming house just outside Keighley, in Yorkshire.

Being still tall and wiry, with unmistakable sharp features when out wearing his tweed deerstalker hat and Inverness cape, whether north or south, meant he was on occasions recognised, stopped – which he put up with, for inevitably Watsons classic write ups of his cases – the collected biography were the real cause of enquiry, although long retired by the sea, the public **will** think of him as still living a frenetic existence holed up at 221B Baker Street with Watson. No chance, all that London smog and traffic, *no thanks*.

By way of diversion that morning Stamford suggested Holmes might like to take the train and visit Haworth – home to the Brontë parsonage – this idea he embraced and was just strolling about on the top of the steep High Street near The Bull pub and town church, when a fellow holding his bowler most respectfully approached.

"Mr. Sherlock Holmes?"

"Indeed."

"Fancy meeting you, might I 'ave a word?"

"Certainly."

"Mr. Perks is the name – I know you're the investigator chappie. I've enjoyed reading them adventures."

"My dear sir, my Baker Street years are long behind me – I am eighty-one this year after all, I am taking life easier, by the sea."

"Aged well Sir, really well, but like I says – I've summat right up your street. Might think it daft at first mind – hey, it's a mighty mystery is this!"

"What mystery exactly?" asked Holmes.

"Ow' a teddy bear came to be strangled, that's wha'." replied Perks.

"Really, that is rather outside my province Mr. Perks. Dear me," Holmes despaired, although not for long - impressed by Mr. Perks chirpy manner and his obvious sincerity, this fellow was not to be put off. No matter what.

A stubborn Yorkshireman, no doubt fond of his

pipe, beer, and cricket he rightly surmised.

"Well, perhaps I can offer wise council at least, although a juvenile matter might surely be better gauged by somebody local – a teacher say. I am but a visitor to Yorkshire after all."

"And welcome 'oop 'ere I'm sure," the fellow glanced at his pocket watch. "Well, me shift starts soon, ave' you a couple of hours t'spare Mr. Holmes? You won't be disappointed, I'd swear it. 'Owt mystery is a mystery, 'an this one is a good 'un alrigh'."

"Very well, I had meant to visit the Brontë parsonage," said Mr. Holmes, casting his eye across the way to the handsome gates surmounting the mossy green steps leading up to the path round the side of the church.

"Nowt goin't anywhere, is it? Parsonage'll still be there when you get back. If you don't mind, we'll take the footpath down t' station – then train ta' Oakworth – the children will be visitin' at midday anyhow. They'll explain better."

"Children?"

"Aye – Roberta, Peter 'n Phyliss, from the three chimneys."

By midday, Oakworth Station was achieved. Mr. Perks changed into his porter's uniform; the old man told to sit tight in the platform waiting room.

How quaint it was. The room carpeted, a warm cheery coal fire in the grate, brass skuttle and fire tongs, a fine pair of polished railway lamps gracing the mantlepiece either side of the mirror.

Puffing on his pipe, the retired consulting detective felt much at home, indeed much impressed by the Great Northern & Southern Railways evident commitment to the comfort of its passengers.

A pannier tank engine hauling a rake of coaches chuffed into the platform, and accompanied by piercing whistles, much steam and smoke later departed.

Five or so minutes passed before the waiting room door slammed open and in burst three beaming children who had just run most of the way from their house.

Mr. Perks encouraged Roberta the eldest, the groups spokesperson to talk openly of their experience.

"You see Mr. Holmes, we're not making this up – please don't think we are."

"Oh, pleeeese don't", emphasised Phylis, making a mocking sorrowful face, glancing across at her younger brother, "It happened yesterday."

"We really did see this." the boy emphasised, cradling a shoe box in his arms.

"You see," continued the eldest girl – all of us were sat on the fence up on the bank near Mytholmes Tunnel as we usually do -the Green Dragon had gone by some time ago, and a little passenger service came next - we had a brilliant view and waved as the train passed."

"The exact time?" asked the retiree, missing nothing.

"Eleven twenty-four," replied Peter confidently.

"Aye, I recall opening the crossing gates," Put in Perks, "down service like."

"Only it was mostly empty at that time of day", the boy pointed out keenly.

"Ugh, how horrid in one of the compartments," Phyllis exclaimed grimacing, "A teddy bear was being strangled, two hands gripping round the poor darling little things neck, shaking the stuffing out."

"Clear as anything through the passing carriage window." Peter finished her sentence.

"An adult?"

"I am certain," answered the eldest girl seriously.

"Humph, the hands grasping the neck no doubt struck you as too large for a child." spoke up elderly Mr. Holmes for now, prepared to humour them. "You were after all Roberta, Peter, and Phyllis three, bonafide witnesses. I suppose doing a violence to anything is fairly unusual in a public space, a moving train and should rightly cause comment. Pray, keep to the facts, enlighten me as to the evidence if any exists."

"Handed in," Mr. Perks butted in. "Go on Peter, show the man". The porter insisted. "A Mrs. Cookson found bits left on't seat in train an' decided it were queer enough t' contact lost property, for despite the state she thought the teddy w'ert brand new."

Holmes did his best to conceal his abject cynicism - watching as the boy opened the lid of the Clarkes shoe box, as if his life depended on it.

Inside the box it was evident the bear had been mangled; material ripped apart with severe force.

Sherlock Holmes instantly put his magnifying lens, mostly used these days for reading small print, to good effect. Studying the debris minutely, already forming in his mind a theory. "Let us observe, pay close attention to the printed gold and blue cloth tag sewn to the left ear. S. Eaves, presumably a manufacturer, else a local toy shop."

"Tha's Haworth's finest, run by Flo Braithwait – Folk swears by Eaves f'ert toys. Wooden tops to model ships n' kiddy prams 'n dolls houses – can be pricey mind."

"Then that establishment is where I am next headed – I am done here – thank you Roberta, Peter and Phyllis – I promise to report later this afternoon, Mr. Perks shall be our liason – yes!"

"Mr. Holmes you will want to retain the shoe box

surely sir?"

"Not at all – lastly," He turned to Mr. Perks the porter, "vital to my enquiry, do you recall observing the frugal smattering of passengers sat in the train that day before whistling out the stopping service from Oakworth station – I shall rely on you to make me a legible list to peruse at leisure."

"Very well Mr. 'Olmes, I'll do me best," said he with a shrug.

———

Mr. Holmes tottered into the toy shop in that charming way elderly folk can muster and promptly ingratiated himself with the proprietor Mrs. Braithwait, who was then serving at the counter.

"My, what a collection of bears – my great

grandchildren should care to own one I'm sure – differing sizes, what stitchwork, what splendid button edges." He gushed unreservedly.

"We're proud of 'em at S. Eaves, made local like. Can I help you sir?" said she, alert to his posh southerner's accent.

"The display is most excellent, and yet, I should really not mention this… but."

"Speak plain, I'm a Yorkshire woman born 'n bred after al'."

"One fears the common shoplifter madam – is your display of teddys not positioned in such a way to attract the low, villainous classes and make easy prey to pilfer?"

"Nay!" she laughed gaily, "I've nowt 'ad no bother sir – bless your concern for our teddys – mind thee, we did 'ave a right fuss t'other day out 'ont street."

"Really, pray enlighten me further," said the retired consulting detective shrewdly, leaning on his ebony cane, scowling through the bowed window at the steep, cobbled hill leading to the top of Haworth, making a mental note of the location, the shops opposite.

"T'were like this see," leaning on the counter Mrs. Braithwait clasped her hands together. "To cut a long story – a fine old gentleman and a little lad came into my shop. Well, Grandpa brought the most expensive teddy in our range. Freddy the Bear, quite the biggest we stock."

"Freddy the Bear," Holmes repeated solemnly.

"Next, e' what a carry on! They w'ert getting int'

horse-drawn Brougham when I swears some blinkin' pickpocket musta' pinched the bear. Who'd do a thing like tha' I ask you – snatch a teddy from a youngster, an' scarper. Ooh, makes me blood boil. Any'ow after I hears the poor little mite sobbin' and' shouts for a policeman. But what can yer do – Fred were the only one left o' his size – nowt right, but there we are."

So, Freddy it must have been, was strangled in the train carriage. The old fellow was more determined than ever to solve *The Worth Valley Mystery*, for he now strongly suspected, however farcical, a more lofty crime was the real intention.

"Mrs. Braithwait, might I intrude and ask if you recognise this?"

Mr. Holmes withdrew from his pocket – the blue

and gold cloth ear tag.

"I do, and ont back 'ere 'n let me have a butchers... yes, the serial number... 0012 – that's Fred alrigh' – Why, I'd like to boil in oil whoever stole that teddy!"

The pace did not relent.

"Allow me to read out loud a list of names. Do you perchance recognise any of the persons?"

"Try me."

"Albert Beggs," began Holmes.

"Farmer chappie – frequents The Bull."

"Flora Sharples."

"Was a millworker 'afore she married. Nice lass."

"Bertha Crowther?"

"Outwardly most respectable, but tha' bitch cons folk out of money, what's rightly theirs... don't we all's know – go's round Worth Valley knockin' at doors. Oh that'a a right bit of old tat, I'll give yer a couple of pence. You know the sort – next it's onto her stall, China sheep or wot-not selling f'ert fifty pound to a dealer. She does a good trade."

"Wears spectacles?"

"Wha' yes, bit short-sighted I believe. See her bric-a-brak stall for yersel' at the regular market oop the hill sir, I must rightly be getting' on. Can I interest thee in one of our teddys for your great grandson p'raps." she smiled sweetly.

"She lives whereabouts?" asked Holmes ignoring her entreaty.

"Why Mrs. Crowther lives out Oxenhope way."

"Good day." Holmes lifted his hat, darting out of the shop. Not daring to glance back – whatever, he now knew all he required to form a competent analysis as to what really happened.

"Mr. Perks," said the elderly man, enjoying a pipe and mug of strong tea in the smokey porters' room at Oakworth station. Rows of railway lamps awaiting a good clean and polish. Holmes' deerstalker hung on the back of a stiff backed wooden, very functional chair.

"Please convey to the children of three chimneys, that I have solved the teddy bear fiasco. A Bertha Crowther living up the line at Oxenhope is the culprit. I stake my reputation on it."

"I'm surprised, that'd be the market stall holder. Me missus had dealings with her once or twice over some ol' tat we wanted rid of. A very sincere, kindly woman if I recall."

"Humph, I beg to differ – a grasping, greedy 'chancer' to my way of thinking."

"Really, wait till I tell the missus," Perks grinned hugely. "'ere, have an iced bun, kiddies brought 'em earlier, whole bag full."

"I will thank you."

Choosing a bun from the plate, the meeting continued. "Upon Monday last, I can report a kindly old gentleman and his grandchild had just come out of the toyshop, when Mrs. Crowther approached – snatching the bear. Able to quickly find anonymity amongst pedestrians, before continuing down the hill to catch her train. This brazen act inspired more than anything else by poor eyesight and a mistaken impulse." The retired consulting detective paused to sip his tea. "For Mr. Perks, she mistook," he continued "Mistook I propose the S. Eaves teddy for the much rarer and more expensive ear studded *Steiffs* product. The bear you may or may not realise commands huge prices among collectors, sold notably in the department stores of London."

"Beyond our means, I'm sure." The porter poured more steaming black Lipton's brew into both mugs from the teapot.

Old Mr. Holmes brushed crumbs off his Inverness cape, further declaring, "boarding the train in her obvious frustration – the market holder having realised her stupendous error took out her despair on the lesser S. Eaves toy, alas throttling and ripping it to shreds in a rage."

"Poor ol' Fred the Ted I say." the porter reflected with a glint in his eye. Tickled that so eminent a figure as the retired detective Sherlock Holmes should have offered his services to The Railway Children.

The Old Man of The Sea

Colonel Hinde's won the first two holes, going steadily ahead to five up. Sherlock won back a couple and went three down. All square by the thirteenth the Colonel blinked, watching Holmes line up his putt, when a distraction occurred.

Both men paused their game gazing skywards, as did other golfers, for clouds had rolled in over the headland, blown off the sea, the English Channel at this time of year decidedly choppy.

Subsequently above Seabury Head Links, the clubhouse that is, could be seen briefly an unusual cloud formation.

A cluster of vapour in the likeness of an old man with a long straggly beard, lasting all but a few minutes before dissolving.

"Was this face in the sky wise old Socrates?" said some wag later at the clubhouse bar, "Else perhaps God himself watching over the links." Whatever, elderly Mr. Holmes went on to win the game and Colonel Hindes paid for lunch.

Pleased by the result, strolling back home along by the post and wire fence bordering the range of cliffs, gulls and crows wheeling out at sea, the sky blustery, the retiree was alerted to the sound of a tinkling bell, thence jangling reins and the clop of hooves coming up behind.

The vicar of Pebblesea, a known personality – the Reverend Lee – doffed his parson's hat cordially before parking his pony trap over by the verge.

"My dear Sherlock," the clergyman called out,

repositioning the reins. "Just on my way to your cottage. Have you perchance an hour or so to spare? If so, clamber up. Most irregular, never seen anything quite like it."

"Really," was all Holmes could muster by way of response while clambering into the yellow cart." Pray, be a trifle more specific."

"The coastguards daughter Mary Firle and Edward Suggs and the ever so tragic circumstances surrounding their deaths I refer to!"

"Naturally – I was the person who first discovered the youth had hung himself inside the lighthouse and gave evidence at the inquest. A sorry business indeed. The girl is now I hear buried quite near the lych gate, the disparate youth on the north side of your Pebblesea churchyard, as is deemed proper."

"Quite Mr. Holmes, in the case of suicide, ecclesiastical law dictates thus. However, I'd value your insight on a most peculiar occurrence. For early this autumnal morning my sexton Tamworth, walking the wheelbarrow over to tend his bonfire became aware of certain ambiguities concerning both of the deceased's graves. Now I'd best shut up on the subject allowing you to form your own wholly unbiased analysis when we presently reach Pebblesea. C'mon Penelope – Hup, hup – briskly now old girl – soon be home."

A tiny bell tinkled on her harness and the white pony trotted off, continuing along a chalk track leading further inland, away from the coast.

———

St. Botolph's Pebbleasea, was a Norman church, chiefly remarkable for ancient mural paintings and a lofty shingle roofed spire.

The vicar was presently guiding an elderly gentleman round the picturesque churchyard. His mind concerned upon relating certain facts of an unsettling nature.

"The lighthouse y'know is reputedly haunted, as legend would have it – by *The Old Man of the Sea*. Apparently, a benevolent entity who claims lost souls, taking them away to some deep oceanic kingdom, overseen by Neptune himself. Alas, upon the seabed he also turns these lost souls into the underwater equivalent of our garden statuary, stone ornaments no less. A charmingly backwards civilisation I'd say."

"Not so benevolent," chuckled the retiree. "To be honest Lee, the only real experience of underwater worlds I possess may be gleaned from my domestic Mrs. Cobb's fish tank – a Grecian temple, Neptune with his trident, bubbles, mermaids, and goldfish. Me, I'd prefer an earthly paradise on dry land."

"Ah, but my dear Sherlock, I brought you here to the churchyard upon a point of puzzlement – cast your eyes onto this recently filled in grave belonging to poor Mary Firle."

"By Jove! That really is most queer," The hawk like features of the silvery haired old fellow became lost in a thoughtful frown – and no wonder – Mary's grave was strewn with oily kelp, strands of seaweed. Not flung in say the crude random way of a vandal bearing a grudge, yet placed most meticulously.

Cockles, muscles, shells of the beach crafted into a wreath, or more probably on closer inspection a crown – the entwined seaweed alike, woven into various emblems. Strange symbols decorating the plot, produced as a birds will its nest, "I wonder who took so much trouble?"

"Who, or maybe more pertinently what." Proposed the clergyman, eyeing the distant lighthouse warily. Whereupon seizing his companions arm he led the elderly gentleman between rows of lichen blotched headstones, way over to the north side whence were the unmarked graves, the more barren plots and the tufty hump of a supposed Tudor plague pit.

"Here be the last resting place of the maladjusted Edward Suggs." The clergyman waded through the wild ungainly grass, swiftly instructing the sign of the cross above a lowly mound of clay. His expression somewhat stern.

At the head of the grave, once more was witnessed the woven crown of kelp, swirling patterns of seashells covered the rest – nimble fingers at work here, what incredible dexterity!

"A most perplexing issue," admitted Sherlock Holmes. "Shame to disturb, no doubt your sexton will shortly want to tidy up."

"Recall the legend – what personage should be associated with such a piteous call of the sea?" asked the vicar in earnest.

"I'd say a local artist, seeking to create a dramatic effect, you know the sort who trawl the beach in the early hours for flotsam. *The Old Man of the Sea* is of course well-known folklore in these parts."

"He existed I am told even before the construction of the lighthouse."

"Granted, the fable kept alive by generations of cottagers sat round the fire with their children on cold winter nights – but *The Old Man of the Sea* as a reality – surely not, however in theory the link with such a mythical being this far inland is not beyond probability, particularly with the haunted lighthouse in plain view."

"How does it go? *The Old Man of the Sea* collects lost souls, takes them to reside for all eternity somewhere in the depths of the English Channel." recalled the vicar.

"More likely warmer climes," Holmes said with a shiver "The Mediterranean I'd wager!"

"Will you be joining us for our annual service in commemoration for those at sea Mr. Holmes? You know, every year we gather round the lighthouse to sing hymns and pray for sailors in their ships."

"With pleasure," answered the old gent, "yet, can one simply forget the unfortunate pair, Mary Firle and the youth Suggs, bound together by a terrible murder – the passions of young love, any romantic love come to that, quite beyond me I'm afraid – ah well."

"My, my – the afternoon's drawing in – time for a cup of Earl Grey tea and a slice of my wife's most excellent seed cake," suggested the Vicar.

"A capital idea," agreed the sprightly eighty-year-old, "A cup of tea would suit, for it has grown quite chilly out here!"

Holmes felt for his trusty pipe and matches in his cardigan pocket, before both men strode off with a hurried step, eager for a warm blast of fire, that and tea and hot buttered crumpets served in the conducive surroundings of the vicarage.

A fortnight later. Stood amongst the crowd of lantern lit faces, gathered outside the church porch, old Mr. Holmes warmly shook hands with the coastguard Mr. Firle and his wife, also their tubby housekeeper Mrs. Nutson whom he recognised.

Other members of the congregation mingled, well wrapped up against the cold – a crisp clear night in prospect.

Wearing full vestments the vicar moved

everyone forwards indicating the choristers wearing cassocks should lead the way. A tassled, embroidered banner and swaying brass crucifix were hauled aloft and off they went.

The cheery murmur of voices, chattering children included, accompanied the lantern lit procession up onto the downs, for this was a family event for all ages to be followed by a fish and chip supper in the village hall.

Walking along beside Mr. Appleby the church warden, Holmes felt in fine fettle, eager to join in the singalong of popular hymns. Good old Watson had declined to attend the service for his current seventy five years young girlfriend Mavis, whilst out walking the dog had slipped and strained her lower back, necessitating looking after her at Horsham…

he would be meeting up with his golfing partner and old Baker Street flat mate at Christmas.

"Let us pray," intoned the vicar, once everybody was gathered around the base of Pebblesea Lighthouse, perched upon the cliff.

Then the church folk joined in with gusto, singing a rendition of a popular hymn. But something unplanned happened, causing both old and young alike to stare open mouthed. Struck quiet in disbelief, for during a rousing chorus the long disused lighthouse had sprung back into activity, casting garish, green rays from the lamp beam, sweeping about the crowd whence a repetitive whirring noise precipitated the top of the lighthouse, the lamp reflector, to spin slowly round and round, detaching itself to become airborne.

Tilting slightly, the trajectory altered, and the hovering module headed straight out to sea into channel waters, where it dived into the bay with a tremendous phosphorous green splash, beneath the waves… and was seen no more.

The children could not have been more excited, and everybody talked of the lightshow event for days after.

No one cared less about the decapitated historic landmark on the cliff.

The Bluebell Special

A train at Sheffield Park had been shunted into sidings by a Terrier class engine - for in one of the clerestory roofed carriages sat stiffly an unidentified gentleman - quite dead.

Dead from a lethal dose of poison.

It was frosty, a bitterly cold day.

Gas lamps along the station approach had been lit for quite some time now.

Despite the best efforts of the police, the man's identity remained a complete mystery.

This prompted the then chairman of the Railway company to visit the elderly, long retired Mr Sherlock Holmes. Now an octogenarian, residing at his downland cottage near Findon - for he had a most radical proposal on offer.

"Dammit! Worth a try - pray what do you think Holmes, is it really credible?"

"I believe so, wonderfully eccentric anyhow, count me in."

"Really?"

"Absolutely."

The proposal was this…

…That Sir Edwin's executive carriage should be converted into a travelling seance room. A circular polished table, with magnetic alphabet letters to keep them in place while the train was in motion.

The Séance Train should start its journey at Sheffield Park and continue along the line to East Grinstead - the exact same route the deceased gentleman should have at some stage embarked upon before his life became extinct.

The idea being to contact his actual spirit and ascertain the manner of death. Was the poison self-administered or forced by the hand of another passenger, say an anonymous passenger or a person well known to him. Maybe the alphabet cards might reveal valuable clues.

"Count me in," repeated Holmes, leaning forward to pat his labrador, "I enjoy travelling on the Bluebell Line, and my dear Sir Edwin - the séance train that is surely a first."

"But this is really a most serious matter, not a day out excursion, we must establish whether a crime has been committed, or not - there will be four of us present, each like yourself, bringing something professional to the table as it were. Mrs Kean, a medium of much repute, myself, you Holmes and the Rev Partridge, who I think you are already acquainted with - like myself, a member of the Physical research society, he resides in my village, West Hoathly."

"Oh, I know of him certainly," the old gentleman finished his tea, draining the final dregs from the cup. Full of admiration for the chairman, and his novel approach to solving the identity of the mystery man on the train.

"Well, if you're in, I'm in, and the others have also shown their willingness to partake. It only remains for me to finalise arrangements with the railway. My personal carriage will be hitched to a normal stopping service and our fingers touching the upturned glass no sooner than the porter blows his whistle. Spirit contact my dear sir, clear and simple contact is all - I am confident we can communicate with the spirit of this poor fellow, and by tracking the exact same location along the Bluebell Line which he at some stage embarked upon that fateful afternoon, may assist us to understand and receive suitable evidence.

"The police as yet, do not have any evidence as to the ticket, a stub, say a return or whatever?"

No railway ticket was found upon his person, nor anywhere in the compartment."

"That in itself is suspicious, tending towards criminal intent - were the staff contacted?"

"All branch stations from Sheffield Park to East Grinstead were telegraphed, but porters are busy fellows when a train arrives, and in all of the platform bustle unless, it's say a local character who regularly uses the stop - it's difficult to identify every passenger."

"Quite so."

Once Sir Edwin had traipsed off to Findon to join his car, Mr Sherlock Holmes warmed his hands in front of the cheery fire, tickled pink by the radical approach of solving a crime on the séance train.

———

heart of the Sussex Weald. Two big, brown, glossy doors lead out onto the platform from the ticket hall, where a good fire heaped with coal burns in the grate. A very welcome sight for any passenger facing the chill, winter weather that day, including old Mr Holmes, Mrs Kean, the Rev Partridge and Sir Edwin.

The esteemed chairman of the railway company had his own personal executive carriage, an ex-observation coach, and many of the passengers hurrying to catch their train that frosty morning, the station canopy patchy white, icy puddles formed at the platforms edge, wondered no doubt why such a swanky carriage should be coupled to a normal stopping service to East Grinstead, but the porter put whistle to mouth, checking doors before the locomotives loud toot toot boomed around the station and with a steady chuff-chuff-chuff the train slowly departed, heading towards Horstead Keynes.

The chairman's carriage pulled away, passing under the black ironwork footbridge decorated with lanterns, smoke billowing back along the train. The special coach interior was plush and well lit, the oval table taking centre stage laid out with magnetic alphabet cards.

Soon as the whistle blew, the four participants connected, placing their fingertips gently on the base of the upturned glass. This was the nervy part. Would an actual genuine contact be made? Or was this going to be a total waste of time?

But no. The seance was to prove positive.

"Spirit, are you there?" asked Mrs Kean. The glass shifted forcefully on the wax polished surface, skimming around.

YES

"We four, three of us members of the Psychical research society of London are here to help. Please indicate whether this is acceptable for you?"

YES

"Most importantly," said Mrs Kean sternly, her eyes set firmly in a chubby pink face, supporting a wobbly chin, never straying from the alphabet cards. "Are you the same person, discovered deceased in a railway compartment at Sheffield Park by a member of public. This must be clarified if we are to proceed."

YES

Sir Edwin looked relieved that contact had been established and asked, "Have you a message for us?"

YES

"Then pray, elaborate, but do not rush, please take your time."

The Rev Partridge poised his HB pencil above a lined notepad, preparing to receive a message from beyond.

The glass tumbler however did not once falter but flew around the table stopping at each relevant letter card defiantly. Succinctly spelling out the word:

S U M M E R L A N D

Old Mr Holmes, who had been distracted by the rolling view out of the sumptuous carriage window was brought up sharp - he felt a pang of recognition, for the word struck a chord - granted, unpleasantly discordant nonetheless, causing him to shiver.

The two coached stopping service rattled along Freshfield Bank, as with a loud blast of whistle the Terrier class loco 'Thunder', was seen bursting under Town Place Bridge, blowing off clouds of steam.

Summerland is a spiritual term, descriptive, perhaps, of the blissful state awaiting those who have passed 'through the veil' and are reunited with their loved ones upon the 'other side'. They enjoy a pleasant rebirth, free from the care and the many, sometimes unendurable trials that beset upon humankind in general.

That said, for those of us still amongst the earthbound and yet to attain such giddy heights, everyday life is an ordained thing, and we must do our best to embrace it wholeheartedly. The sudden demise of her husband, a man whom she had always loved and admired, must have prompted Mrs Staplehurst to embrace the Summerland concept perhaps a little before time, for aconite is one of the most effective poisons known to science.

The last, unsent letter to Mrs Cobbs, written in a resolved and meticulous neat hand, shortly before Mrs Staplehurst took her own life, contained many references to spiritualism and her recent conversion to it. She suggested her friend should contact the Village Society and become acquainted with the principles and teachings of its founder, Marjo Stallo. Mrs Cobbs had lost no time in showing the letter to old Mr Holmes.

The old gentleman abandoned polishing his violin and examined the letter closely.

"I recall Mrs Staplehurst, on her death, bequeathed a great deal of her husband's personal fortune to the society." Holmes said, tossing the letter aside.

"Well," replied the home help, "that is surely a matter of her own free choice and should be left unquestioned."

After dinner, Holmes picked up the newspaper and sat back in his armchair. "Hereditary," murmured he from behind his broadsheet. "The Earl of Monkton gone. Well, his will shall, no doubt, be bitterly contested by his surviving brother and become the subject of lengthy and drawn-out litigation! Halloa! What the devil?"

The obituary column in The Times had evidently yielded some further intrigue for he folded the paper, underlined a small section in ink, and tossed it across to Mrs Cobbs.

"What do you make of that?" said he, striking a match and lighting his pipe.

She studied the obituary page carefully. There was a small advertisement, which read:

Rejoined. Reunited.

Tell the good news. There is no death.

Sceptics belonging to all creeds, harken. The Village Society can prove beyond all shadow of a doubt that the Summerland truly exists, and life begins anew upon the other side. 'How wonderful realising my dearest husband did not leave me after all and we are to be reunited in the Summerland, whence we shall enjoy a happy and industrious life together. I am forever indebted to the Village Society for their guidance and my only wish is that others should benefit likewise.

Lydia Marchmount,

Lewes

"Tell the good news. There is no death. This I do daily. The village Society has placed me regularly in touch with my beloved wife who now resides in the Summerland. Oh, what joy, and to think, I shall soon be joining her and my arthritis healed.

Mr Albert Marsh

Pebblesea

Those recently bereaved, wishing to seek further information, should apply in writing to: The Village Society

Lewes

When Holmes investigated the village society in Lewes, it proved as bogus as anything and the medium Margo Stallo a complete fraudster – she was later forced out of business by a senior detective Mr Cummings and Mr Holmes's own evidence.

All persons present were aware of what the word *Summerland* implied, only Mr Holmes understood the more criminal usage, but kept this more to himself. Strangely he was warming immensely to this unknown, invisible presence and longed to address the glass by a Christian name, be more civil, have some image of the person when alive.

The stopping service slowed down, it was entering Horstead Keynes with its newsagents kiosk and station canteen - a large station with quite a bustle of people waiting along the platform.

There was the squeal of brakes as 'Thunder' approached, and the train came to a standstill.

The train might have become stationary, but the glass tumbler had become noticeably more animated. The four participants being forced to press firmly as it would skid around. Whatever, in a surprisingly short time a most intriguing alphabet message revealed itself.

Holmes trusted his unfailing intuition and now believed he at last had an inkling of the dead man's occupation.

"You are (or were) I'd say - a retired librarian, a first-rate Times crossword puzzle solver."

C.	E.	J.	R.	S.	G.
D.	G.	A.	H.	L. F.	E.
N.	G.	H.	F.	E.	M.
O.	H.	M.	E.	N.	S.

YES

"Your previous message refers to a code - the initials of famous authors in the public mind - C D for instance, refers to Charles Dickens."

YES YES – IN LIFE I WAS MR LENTILE FROM CAMDEN.

The glass slowed to a standstill and the spirit remained unresponsive to any further questioning - it was therefore decided by Sir Edwin to pause and have an interval for refreshment. This naturally allowed elderly Mr Holmes and the Padre to work out the code. While they sat huddled in a corner exchanging pencil notes, Mrs Kean and Sir Edwin chatted on the sofa, watching the woodland scenery fly by from the large viewing window. Wispy clouds of smoke from the Terrier class engine up front, blew back.

Once the code was determined, Mr Holmes and the vicar did their best to hide their initial reactions, keeping up a front, for now the situation on the train had changed, become far more serious for the provided puzzle was no mere frolic, an entertainment, but a dire warning, the spirit of the deceased mystery man on the train made it plain as a pikestaff.

Dickens Austen Nesbitt Gaskill Engels Ryder-Haggard

Henty Oliphant LeFanu Mayhew Elliot Shelley

Keats Elliot Austen Nesbitt

Sir Edwin's Secretary Hugh Morley, a most estimable and sensible fellow, wheeled in a tea trolley heaped with plates of cakes and sandwiches, fresh scones, jam and clotted cream.

Sir Edwin, ever the perfect gentleman asked Mrs Kean, what took her fancy, but was politely rebuffed.

"I say, one moment," Holmes realised the lady was coming over. "Oh, my dear sir, your lips are so chapped, allow me to offer my own special remedy against the stuffy, dry air, heat generated by the railway engines hot water system," a pair of large brown eyes behind pebble lensed spectacles loomed closer. Held before his face now, a smokey glassed cosmetic pot. Her outstretched finger dabbed with greasy balm rapidly approached his lower protruding lip…

…however, the ever-wily Mr Holmes was not altogether sold on her act. He saw in an instant of supposed kindness only agonising death. Stomach restricting nausea, a burning throat.

The Sheffield line, or the Bluebell Line as it was affectionately called by locals, flew past the carriage window while Holmes, still spritely in his advancing years, seized Mrs Kean's wrist, bending back the lady's finger, causing the lip moisturiser to tumble harmlessly onto the carpet of the carriage. He smothered her hand with a handkerchief - neutralising all chance of her applying the deadly concoction in any way whatsoever.

Mrs Kean blustered and struggled, restrained by Sir Edwin and his secretary.

"Behold, your true colours madam," said old Mr Holmes, regaining his composure while brushing himself down.

The reverend Partridge was not slow to justify his colleagues' dramatic intervention.

"Poison gentlemen - the lip balm contained strychnine, else some filthy derivative - quick acting I'll be bound - once, on the saliva and in your mouth, you're a gonner."

"Although naturally Mrs Kean," smirked old Mr Holmes, rubbing his beaky nose with a forefinger, "we should never in a million years suspect your good self should we my dear, the food, else a digestive ailment perhaps, chronic heartburn, but mark my words Sir Edwin, I should not have lasted the train journey to East Grinstead - and been pronounced dead on arrival at the station. An actress, a mistress of disguise, one Marjo Stallo, a competent fraudster. Now Mrs Kean - who do we really have here I wonder?"

"You and that detective Mr Cummings ruined my expanding 'Summerland' business, left me penniless - it has taken me years to recover - when I heard of your involvement, I was passionate that you should die."

"And like many before Mrs Kean, you thought you could get away with murder - the method, I grant you, unique and utterly brilliant."

"My dear Holmes." Protested Sir Edwin, "She just tried to kill you old man."

―――――

The retired librarian was eventually traced by the police to Camden town.

A diary entry proved most enlightening. A relationship began in a pub, led to that same gentleman lending money for printing cards and letterheads to support a Mr Pearce Chope's small but developing business as a tour guide. The friendship proved lasting and Mr Lentile, now in his seventies, decided on a whim to make a will, very

very favourable to his young friend leaving all monies, and worldly goods - property and so forth to:

Dear Pearce,

My rock and my true friend

The entry concludes tellingly.

'I am going on a short break to Sussex by train. I'll pick one of those boarding houses along the front. Plenty of walks on The Downs. Pearce told me that he is rather busy at present. That's a shame, writing his Magnum Opus, 'Haunted Places on the London Underground', he'll look after the cat for me anyhow.'

But it ended up he looked after a lot more than that.

―――――

The Pebblesea Murders

Following the Séance Train Puzzler was a relatively quiet time for old Mr Holmes on the crime front – he continued to enjoy his golf, partnered by Dr Watson, shopping in the village and taking the dog for a walk.

Come August Mr Sherlock Holmes was invited by the vicar of Brambledean to accept the offer of a talk at the village hall, tea and biscuits served - questions and answers, absolutely no publicity, a very informal local affair word of mouth - the event packed anyway, the Baker Street years, always a matter of interest to members of the public.

The retiree himself preferred to keep a low profile, but on this occasion agreed to share a light-hearted personal view of his time spent sharing a flat with friend Watson in London's Marylebone, plus various anecdotes from past adventures, mention of Professor Moriarty and the Hound of the Baskerville's, always popular with audiences.

Holmes was gratified to see certain personages he had lately helped in his own unique way in retirement. Front row, the crime writer Falcon smith, whom he discovered was being hypnotized by his fellow author Mrs Alcott from Sumpting when silverware was mysteriously disappearing from a locked cabinet, then there, dotted amongst the stalwart 'Brambledeaners' like Mrs Simpkins from the Mews, was his near neighbour Sally Sudbury, a

Mr Winstanley the prize marrow grower, Mrs Long and her wonderfully inventive daughters from afar field as Henfield, further juveniles represented by the Railway children Bobbie, Phyllis and Peter come up specially from London with mother and father, memorable for the 'Worth Valley Mystery'.

The talk was received well, alas disappointingly on this occasion at the village hall questions and answers about to round off, a local ironmonger Mr Firth, got up and would harp on about beekeeping, and how were Holmes' hives thriving, how many pounds of pure sweet honey produced.

He tactfully checked his watch. "Nowadays golf is my abiding interest, I have not for many years been involved with that particular line - I can however recommend a first rate book by A. L. Selby, a much greater bee enthusiast than I ever was - I believe tea and biscuits are about to be served."

After the talk Holmes was inundated with well-wishers, spending much time chatting with eager members of the audience.

A very determined Mrs Simkins, a lady who lived along the winding cliff road at The Mews with her scientist husband and little dog, approached the edge of the stage, cup of tea in hand.

"Why Mrs Simkins," Holmes enthused, "I recall with fondness, our last encounter, The Mews being a centre of multiple robbery, I trust you are well, and how pray is that dear old deaf lady Mrs Wright, who practically solved the case by way of a simple gesture?"

"Buried in Brambledean churchyard Mr Holmes."

"I see."

"Y'know Mr Holmes, no one could ever replace her as a resident. Her little face peering out of the window - 'Queen of the Mews', we called her."

"I remember you saying, ah, the vicar approaches - first rate question of yours Padre concerning John Hebron of Atlanta in one of my more obscure cases 'The Yellow Face'. You are hereby dubbed my honorary Dr Watson. The good doctor is of course on holiday in Egypt with his current female acquaintance – a Mrs Claudia Ledbury, not due back until the end of the week."

"Why thank you Holmes! I am more than qualified for that post - you will recall I keep a complete set of your Paget illustrated biography in my study."

"Police! Stand aside." Barked a gruff voice. Certain members of the audience rattling cups and saucers cleared a path. A pair of quizzical tea ladies manning the urn glanced up from the hatch.

"Oh bother," said the vicar, raising his eyebrows in mock theatrical concern, "What have we here? Peg selling tickets on the door, fingers in the till?"

Holmes, upon seeing the policeman's approach, removed his pipe from his tweed coat before beginning to fill it.

"Beg pardon Vicar, Sgt Froggins - Mr Sherlock Holmes," he raised an awkward half salute, "the ornithologist Sandy Johnson."

The retiree noticeably stiffened, "Potholes? Cycle accident? Fell off of that perishing penny farthing he rides showing off to everyone - Eastbourne hospital, is it? The old boy's alright, isn't he?"

"Worse by far - looks like a murder Sir." The officer hung his head in a sombre expression.

"Murder. But that's absurd."

"Mr Holmes your presence is required on the Downs. The body was discovered two hundred yards or so from Pebblesea Lighthouse."

"Oh that," spoke up Mrs Simpkins, "The American industrialist Dr Meecham bought Pebblesea Manor last year, didn't he? Now he's decided to buy the old Lighthouse ruin as well, to renovate it. Alright for some, pots of money. Still owns steel mills and chemical plants in

Pennsylvania - a very wealthy chap so we're told by The Echo. C'mon Sarge, any more details? Can't get much worse cannit?"

"None worse than murder ma'am," Sgt Froggins remained tight lipped.

Holmes knew Sandy fairly well. Saw him out and about on the cliffs, studying the grey nape jackdaw that had over time interbred with the carrion crow population of the vicinity. Both groups living quite happily alongside the gull colony - they'd been chatting about that very topic only last week at Seabury Head.

"Tell me, who's in charge?" Holmes asked despairingly, "No bunglers on this one. Chisholm of Brighton force is competent, Inspector Yardley a better bet though." He drew a heavy sigh.

"Inspector Wilson," Froggins coughed gruffly, "young fella, a while back transferred then rose through the ranks."

"Ah, young Wilson, good golfer, fair handicap, seen him on the links - an officer of promise so long as he takes his time and heaven forbid, never…"

"A student of your methods Sir, the body has not yet been moved, the immediate area cordoned off - the h'inspector wished me to convey that you'll find no fault on that account."

The vicar's wife Pru quickly conveyed the latest developments to those assembled in the village hall, who found the whole police intervention very in keeping with the talk that had taken place previous to that.

Mrs Simpkins barged in front, "Oh, might I accompany you Mr Holmes?" She said importantly and with much determination. Not taking no for an answer. "My husband is looking after Freddy, my dog, I am not expected back for quite a while."

"And I," added the Padre good humouredly, "I can act as your stand in Doctor Watson - seriously Mrs Simkins I was in the war. I think Sgt Froggins should agree a murder scene's no place for a lady."

"The body is not a pretty sight ma'am. You probably won't be allowed near the investigation scene."

"Oh, I'm not having that. You jolly well try and stop me - I'm not about to faint at the first sight of blood - a weak helpless female is it? For you bullish chaps to fuss over."

"Is there any room in the car Sgt?" Enquired Holmes with a withering glance, hurriedly gathering his stout ash walking stick, deerstalker hat and Inverness cape. Sgt Froggins indicated the affirmative.

Blinding bright sunshine and the sound of traffic met the group as quitting the memorial hall, they emerged onto Brambledean High Street. A black Alvis saloon reversed at speed, mounting the pavement.

Everyone got inside the patrol car, which was capable of a very respectable ninety miles an hour, and whizzed off along past the quaint tearooms and shops of Brambledean.

Once out of town they turned left at the junction onto the undulating coast road, a cooling breeze encircling the back seat passengers from the partly open window.

The smock windmill above the village was soon left in the distance, as the official motor accelerated round the side of a country bus following the cliff route. The grassy ridge of coast overlooking rocky outcrops and the glistening blue waters of the English Channel.

The village of Pebblesea with its charming turreted Norman church was eventually attained, the saloon car shifting gears, bumped and wound its way up a stoney track leading on towards the high downs. Those bracing open heights being home ground for walking the labrador, old Mr Holmes knew the area intimately.

Seen across the way Dr Meecham's restoration project, the lighthouse, was shrouded by tarpaulin and scaffolding - loud hammering, grinding drills - a building works in progress.

A group of police on the other side of the furze and clumps of thicket glanced around at their approach. Once the Alvis had parked, a young detective came over to open the passenger door, recognising the familiar deerstalker, but totally unprepared for the vivacious lady powdering her nose from a handbag compact.

"This, is my acquaintance Mrs Simpkins and of course, you know the vicar of Brambledean," said Holmes with a nod.

"Glad to meet you ma'am. I'm afraid in the case of a serious crime I am bound to follow strict protocol, the regulations are firm. Vicar, perhaps you could accompany the lady behind the rope over there by the path? Mr Holmes, please step this way." The officer said with due gravitas.

The sheeted remains over the way resembled not too unkindly a beached seal amongst the gorse. A gust of in shore breeze made the covers flap - a constable duly removed the sheet, and Holmes peering over the detective's shoulder was witness to the appalling injuries, the body terribly broken about.

"We assume Mr Johnson was out walking, perhaps last evening," remarked Inspector Wilson. "Where he was met with a likely unprovoked attack. It's brutal I mark you, one of the worst I've ever seen."

Mr Sherlock Holmes stooped down removing his deerstalker hat, "Poor old Sandy, to end like this. He was such a kind, gentle and considerate fellow - a fine author of birding books of which I have a number of autographed copies. No enemy in the world I can think of - who'd do such a thing?"

"Do you require a magnifying lens? I have one in my police bag Mr Holmes."

"Splendid, an officer after my own heart - good putter, I've seen you on occasions at Seabury Head links I'll be bound, you pair with Jenkins. What was in his possession?"

"Nothing of value, no wallet or pocket watch."

"Well say notebook, pencils, birding net, pipe, box of matches, toffee foils."

"Nothing whatsoever Sir."

Old Mr Holmes after running the magnifying lens down one side of the victims swollen face, got up, allowing for a cursory inspection of the immediate vicinity.

"Found the weapon yet? I'd say a hefty, large cudgel, something with swing."

"We'll keep looking, don't worry."

"Look here Wilson - let's suppose there was more than one person involved in the attack, say a case of mistaken identity may arise by a person who was in drink - gracious whoever did this must have been livid with rage, frenzied, to think it could have been me instead of him laying down there - out walking the dog - I dare not conceive."

"We're looking into all possibilities Sir – no stone shall remain unturned."

"Well, I'll leave you to it Inspector, I'm done. Now to visit Sandy's cottage further up to see whether any clues exist to his last movements. Dear Mrs Simkins and the vicar must be feeling rather put out by now, but I'm sure my team'll prove useful.

"I'm certain they will," the inspector replied with a wry smile, "I'm honoured to have met you Mr Holmes - your time and unique talents are much appreciated by the Sussex Police Force."

"Sandy was not exactly close, but a neighbour - I'll not rest until this filthy killer is hung, I can tell you Wilson - the locals will be devastated."

The victim's home was an old labourer's homestead, delightfully restored, a flint cottage with tiled roof, chunky brick chimney stack at one end - green painted windows and doors, presently (at the height of summer) left ajar - folk of this region were open and hospitable, the wayfarer, the coastal walkers welcome to fill their water bottles from the tap in the cottage garden, which was now resplendent in its full bloom and glorious colours.

Somewhat sadly, Johnson's lethal penny farthing, propped round the side. How Sandy enjoyed defying gravity, being perched on his tiny seat atop of that big front wheel, doffing his cap from a height at the ladies while trundling along. The inside of the cottage met with general approval - plenty of horse brasses and rustic furnishings.

Putting the kettle on, gathering cups and saucers Mrs Simpkins felt quite at home - the place being cheery and comfortable.

Meanwhile Holmes and the vicar visited first, the upstairs - then the lower rooms. Of note, the ornithologist's study, a real writer's haven, with an author's nook, full of books and sketch pads. Everything crowded in delightfully in a hap hazard characterful way. Stuffed birds under glass, cricket bats, with fishing rod and tackle. Basket clutter, quirky knick knacks in a row atop of the mantelshelf - a nice desk with a window view of the sea and the promontory lighthouse.

Elderly Mr Holmes felt more drawn however, to a narrow back room next to the pantry, that smelt of freshly seasoned wood, wherein was a workbench littered with boxes of tacks, sandpaper and a rack of woodworking tools.

The Padre was quick to join his companion and

pass comment, "Now, I should be inclined, acting as your temporary doctor Watson to theorise, that this fellow builds model sailing ships - the evidence is clearly laid out before us - lengths of doweling, two by two ply, rolls of cloth, a pot of glue, naughty naughty - brush left to harden there see."

"What about kite building?" suggested Mrs Simpkins popping her head round the door.

"Referring to flying kites, I never in my life, walking the dog on a windy day even saw him gazing aloft tugging at one. Sandy's abiding passion was for watching birdlife through his binoculars, making nature notes for his next book - a first-rate observer of habitat."

The Padre gave a shrug, and raised his hands, "Don't look at me Mr Holmes, I am a hundred percent certain Mr Johnson was a modeller - alright, not toy boats then, but something along those lines."

"Let us consider the facts," Whilst sat down having their tea Holmes, as of yore, steepled his long boney fingers together, forming a pyramid. Mrs Simkins leaned forward, as did the clergyman. "This is a brilliant reminder how we must think outside of the parameters of initial impressions. We have rolls of sailcloth treated with chandlers' resin, thus coated to be water resistant, stretchable and very tough wearing. We have boxes of tacks, sheets of sandpaper, a congealed pot of specialist wood adhesive, a stack of doweling rods, and 2 by 2 ply - all of this could feasibly be used to part construct a small dingy or say a coracle - one of those simple round neolithic affairs. In short, not just model ships, we are dealing with the possibility of a more substantial craft, contributing in some way to the overall design. But all of this is totally out of character, he was hardly a boating enthusiast spending his days out on the harbour jetty. Look here now Simkins, you and the vicar had best take the coastal bus back to Brambledean. I intend to dwell on this little problem over a pipe of Ogden Walnut Sliced tobacco back at home. That is. After a roast dinner served by the most excellent Mrs Cobbs - don't sulk so Mrs Simkins, we must remain civil, and I promise wholeheartedly to keep you both informed."

"Informed - I see, a police way of shunting us out of the picture, I do own a motorcycle and sidecar, y'know Sherlock - *murder done will travel* - goodness

I'm due to take a service at seven - we'd better get to the bus stop - Flintingdon is only down the way - the number twelve's pretty frequent."

"How I fondly recall the hair-raising occasion when you gave me a lift over to Brambledean doing 75mph practically all of the way! Good heavens, those tight bends. Very well, I'll expect you both at my place at nine o' clock - independent transport is no bad thing, and being over eighty now, I could do with a little help," admitted the old gentleman.

Before everyone left, a further question was forthcoming. Once again, Mrs Simpkins proved her razor-sharp intellect more than a match for the ageing Mr Holmes, who took his hat off to her.

"Are we not ignoring a further part of the equation, that being - were the injuries sustained by

Mr Johnson, consistent with say, falling off his penny farthing, that silly old death trap of his." She washed up the tea things in the sink.

"My dear young lady, that… is a very astute point. From what I gather though, he had learnt over time to fall like a circus acrobat - Sandy did indeed fall off on occasions, but with his training managed to get away with scuffed shins and grazes - No Mrs Simpkins, what we have back there is a serious case of assault, of much greater severity."

Taking the coastal path along by the cliffs past Berwick Gap, towards Seabury Head, the retiree Sherlock Holmes, trusty stick in hand veered off at a settled pace towards Findon. Arriving home at around six of the clock, to be met on the step of Horseshoe Cottage by his soppy labrador. Mrs Cobbs was busy in the kitchen preparing dinner. After making a suitable fuss of the dog, Holmes made straight to the crystal cut decanter on the Welsh dresser and had only just poured himself a liberal measure of 'Olde Hogmanay' single malt, when a firm rap on the horseshoe door knocker announced the arrival of an unexpected guest.

A Mr Exeter, who until that time was a complete unknown to him. A proffered business card revealed the person to be the partner of Doctor Meecham, the wealthy industrialist himself.

Passing by in his dogcart through the village, Exeter confessed, being an American, having read all of the published cases in Lippincott's magazine, he just had to meet in person the great Mr Holmes and could not resist calling at the cottage.

Entertained by a glass of Scotch, Exeter talked on various topics, most notably was this visitor mortified by the apparent lack of SHERLOCKIANA as he called it in the cottage. Fully expecting a framed portrait of Reichenbach Falls taking pride of place above the mantlepiece. Much more evidence of significant memorabilia, for instance the Persian slipper, Watson's old service revolver kept glorified behind glass, the famous stemmed cherrywood pipe, worth how many thousands of pounds now?

Elderly Mr Holmes was adamant all the Baker Street clutter had long gone to the London sale rooms, else Greens Emporium in Henfield.

The fellow in a state of disbelief emphasised Dr Meecham should have paid a small fortune for any item related to Baker Street, but this said as the table was laid, a broad hint was cast by Mrs Cobbs that dinner was ready. The pair ended their conversation cordially enough with cheerful goodbyes, a pause to pat the dog which far from the usual endearing wag of its tail growled perceptively.

There was the promise of a future meeting at the manor.

"Beg pardon sir," said Mrs Cobbs, spooning a large portion of steak and kidney pie onto his plate. "I don't mean to be rude, but I can't help myself, what a peculiar head that man Exeter had."

"Granted Mrs Cobbs, one considers geometry, drawing the face as an upside-down triangle - on the reversed apex we have a chiselled chin and small cruel mouth."

"Wide, set apart goggly eyes, high cheekbones resembling gills - no eyebrows to speak of. E's head like an upturned cereal bowl."

"You've got it in one Mrs Cobbs - my dog didn't seem to take very kindly to Mr Exeter did you boy."

———

Later that evening Sherlock took the dog on their usual evening walk, with a firm resolve to revisit the murder scene further along the coast, a clear bright moon, the Parish Lantern as it was called in the old days, assisted his purpose admirably.

For him being alive and in good health down to the fresh sea air and exercise, striding across the firm downland turf was just the ticket, yet for poor deceased Sandy Johnson, stiff and motionless, only mortuary proceedings beckoned. The marble slab, the prospect of autopsy, so catching his killer, bringing whoever to face justice, was uppermost.

Upon reaching the area, it was evident a low sprawl of furze and bracken offered little hiding place for a villain, unless they were lying face down. Holmes began strolling up and down keeping a look out for any flattened vegetation when his dog came running up, between its jaws a snapped piece of doweling - attached to a fragment of treated sailcloth, being both tacked and glued in place. He shifted his gaze in the direction of the lighthouse. Scaffolding and sheets of tarpaulin lit up by the moon some 200 yards distant.

Upon returning home, the old fellow seized open the door of a broom cupboard stacked to the gunnels with labelled bundles of old newspaper editions - The Times, The Telegraph were on this occasion dismissed, The Sussex Echo however, some hundred and thirty weekly issues the preferred choice. Pouring himself a stiff Rabbie Burns, he prepared himself for a marathon search that should last into the wee hours.

The following morning proved eventful, not only did Mrs Simkins and her uncommon little dog Freddy arrive, together with the vicar roaring up on his smoky motorbike and sidecar, but earlier Inspector Wilson had called, being fussed over by

Mrs Cobbs to partake of a substantial breakfast of ham and eggs. Which he was in sore need of.

For barely is one serious murder announced than another topples atop of it. The Sussex constabulary called out at six am, to investigate a similar case of violent death down in the dip where the village green, the fine old houses and cottages, and church of St Botolph's, Pebblesea, had nestled for centuries. One of the characteristic little towns and villages which lie so invitingly snug under the shadow of the hills.

The forensic elements were similar.

A brutal killer, striking unseen upon two different occasions.

The body, that of a solicitor, Mr Chalfont Daly with a practice in Firle Place, a long-time resident of the tight knit Downland community, battered to death on a grass verge bordered by dry-stone walling. On the other side of the wall, a strip of wheatfield, the parish church in easy view.

The fatality was discovered by an early morning milkman on his rounds.

No sooner did the inspector polish off his last slice of wholemeal toast than he pleaded with the eighty-year-old Holmes then agreeably filling his pipe before striking a swan vesta match, to accompany him back to the murder scene. Blowing out blue wreaths of tobacco smoke Holmes politely declined, explaining he was presently awaiting Mrs Simkins and the Rev Peter Armitage on his powerful motorbike, to arrive from over at Brambledean. He offered his assurance he should catch up with the police investigation by half nine.

"The body must be kept in exactly the same position in which it was found, nothing disturbed - the tiniest upsetting of the grass by clumsy boots may lose a significant clue. You know my methods, act on them, oh and pray - what do you make of this? Moving the toast rack and coffee pot aside, the old gentleman passed across a piece of snapped doweling rod affixed, a fragment of sail cloth - tacked and glued to the wood.

"No idea Sir." Came the response.

―――――

A half hour after the Inspector had quit the cottage for his patrol car parked in Findon, the vicar's hand grasped the throttle of his motorcycle combination, the machine revved and trembled, issuing smoky exhaust fumes across the flower tubs.

Mrs Simkins made certain that Holme's deerstalker was tied firmly beneath his chin, his Inverness cape secured against the fierce wind of the motorbike.

Waving them off from the honeysuckle porch was Mrs Cobbs, dishcloth in hand, labrador barking playfully at his newfound woolly-headed friend.

Whilst the (semi) retired consulting detective rode pillion, sat aside the Sinclair-Alco 500cc machine, the redoubtable lady of the Mews Mrs Simkins crouched in the springy sidecar with her dog, who enjoyed fast and furious travel, woofing merrily as the motorbike and sidecar roared off in search of Pebblesea village.

The second murder scene more than matched the notoriety of the first, the solicitor beaten about, fractured bones - a frenzied attack most likely launched by a madman bearing a hefty cudgel.

As was his way, Holmes persisted with his obtuse questioning.

"Were Mr Lawson's pockets empty?"

"No valuables whatsoever."

"Not even a pipe or matches, a propelling pencil, petrol lighter, coins?"

"None of that."

"Well then, that tells us an awful good deal. Surely, if a chap's taking a stroll around the village he keeps loose change in his pocket - some basic personal effects. The solicitor, from what Sgt Froggins gleaned must have been out very late. For nobody recalls seeing him. This is all adding up to something indeed… now where's my team, ah Padre, Mrs Simkins, would you do me the honour of using this tape measure please. My, the sun is strong. One of you stand at the base of the church tower, the other, unravel, taking your direction from where the body is currently located. Aim for a straight line and see how many yards exist between it and the tower itself. Yes, I realise the headstones and flint wall get in the way but let's roughly pace it out, I'd gun for about one sixty yards to the verge we're stood on. Officers, I want you to painstakingly search either side of the line checking the ground meticulously. Inspector Wilson and I shall do likewise. Sergeant Froggins, a word in your ear if I may. I have a special job for you – draw me a small diagram of the immediate area in your notebook. Church tower to wheat field, got that?"

At one o' clock, when it was about time to adjourn to the Crooked Billet for a ploughman's lunch - the body having since been removed by horse ambulance, Mrs Simkins came running up, her face the picture of rapture, for just while everyone was tiring to the task (most regarding it to be a waste of police time) fed up with looking for what? She had kept on with the search. As had Freddy, her equally committed pooch, and been rewarded for latterly, she knelt down in the wild grass and recognised something familiar.

Elderly Mr Holmes felt rightly vindicated, had since his discovery the evening before held out just such a possibility, now it had happened for Mrs Simkins clutched between the fingers of her outstretched hand - items of terrific moment, consider, a snapped 'L' shape doweling rod, a shard of 2 by 2 ply, sail cloth coated with chandler's resin, glued in place yet bent asunder by catastrophic impact.

Lifting up Freddy the dog with a cuddle she exclaimed, "Holmes you old fox, you're onto something, I know it!"

"What a bally corker!" the Padre was of a like mind, recognising the items and their significance. Part of a wooden structure, but what exactly?

Inspector Wilson, along with other officers, gathered round, but could see nothing remotely of serious significance. Indeed, certain senior ranks were becoming increasingly annoyed at what they saw was a complete waste of police time involving a doddery old fool, a silly young woman and the 'clingy' cleric.

———

Breezy cumulus cloud was skimming across the sky above the coastal village.

Taking full advantage of the rapid Sinclair-Alco - three individuals and dog puttered along the sunny High Street, thence over a fording bridge, turning left up a lane to reach ultimately an imposing manor house, that for centuries held sway over the land for miles around, the church and the big house supposed guardians of the spiritual and social welfare of the community.

"So have you solved the double murders then?" Shouted Mrs Simkins over the roar of the motorbike's engine, "you were terribly cagey with the officer in charge back there."

Holmes twisted round to face her, "Learn carefully what I relate once we're inside the manor house my dear. Yesterday, back at the village hall, Mr Hardcastle couldn't praise your interior decoration skills enough - you completely refurbished the Kempton apartments in Brighton I hear - a most excellent occupation for what it is I have in mind."

"I must admit that I do show quite a talent in that line."

"A superlative ruse beckons, your task being to ingratiate yourself to Dr Meecham, and if you are fortunate enough to be shown around the house by the butler, or whoever greets you, take careful note of any discrepancies - your keen eye for decorating may come in very handy. Bits of paper people tend to leave around, drawers left open, important documents - you know the score. The Padre and I on the other hand shall concern ourselves wholly with the American incumbent Dr Meecham."

"Those of us acquainted with English history Dr Meecham recall a certain monk in the eleventh century, Elmer by name, who constructed wings for arms and legs to attain sufficient buoyancy to fly. He attained this by launching himself off of a tower, flapping manually he managed to glide hundreds of yards before crashing to the ground, fracturing both legs. Does this remind you of certain recent events?"

"I have no idea what it is you are talking about Mr Holmes. Time for an interlude, drink anyone?"

There was the whirring of clockwork, or was it the humming of a battery, before in came, accompanied by Exeter, a remarkable Paget like mobile mannequin of a young Sherlock Holmes. Wearing a deerstalker, Inverness cape and bearing a tray of glasses, "God knows gentlemen, everybody needs an animatronic Sherlock Holmes to give one a decent back rub – or say cook up a good old bubble and squeak. A life essential wouldn't you say. Pour out three glasses of neat scotch please." the automaton did as was requested; Exeter close by at all times.

"One of Exeter's advanced Meccano builds."

"Well, that's confoundedly smart." Praised the Padre, caught quite off guard.

"Furthermore," continued Holmes, not missing a beat, "in order to have a competition of this nature, there are bound to be strict rules - plans were presumably supplied to both parties - for a pair of identical wing structures to be built by the competitors themselves, keeping rigidly to the Elmer formula. The person deemed to have flown manually over the greatest distance should be judged the winner, beating that original 200 yards achieved by the monk of old himself. Johnson was first to make the attempt and failed. The village solicitor the second aeronaut to take part. Make no mistake, the nature of each man's flight was the only means of obtaining the considerable prize money put up by yourself to launch the competition - even so, the solicitor went ahead, fully knowing his sporting challenger lay dead asunder, critically injured upon the downs. Alas, we know, he too, succumbed to the icarus syndrome, what have you to say Dr Meecham? Two men have since died, and yet you appear little troubled."

"How then Mr Holmes, and you too Padre, did I become acquainted with these men? I have never met them before in my life. This ridiculous notion of chucking yourself off and out into thin air, what's his name? Elmer?"

Dr Meecham gazed on the pair with wry amusement - the moving mechanical device in the image of young Mr Holmes clunkily delivered the drinks, before meekly exiting the room. The original consulting detective did not but bat an eyelid. He had observed similar working automata at the great Crystal Palace exhibition while visiting Upper Norwood with Watson some years ago.

"What could be simpler, you recruited them from back issues of the Sussex Echo, easily enough obtained. By scanning through the various editions, your eyes fell on the first suitable candidate."

"Oh, did I now? Seems to me I am being accused of crimes here that I did not commit. You have not a single dime's worth of proof that implicates me in any way anyhow - give up Mr Holmes, you are beaten, my New York lawyers would crush you old man. They would squeeze every last ounce of your remaining retirement fund, so you would end up a hobo. Don't ever cross me ole' buddy ole' pal. Hey vicar, what about you? Fancy a new lead roof for the old church? I can pay plenty my man."

"You undoubtedly resourced this from a local newspaper - I mean then a second recruit followed, after all who should be able to resist the vast amount of dollars you were offering in prize money? Let alone the chance of competing for manual flight! You Dr Meecham, as I did learn from various articles chose Chalfont Lawson, a person amongst a small lottery of crackpots, who had on a number of occasions jumped off the end of Brighton pier, equipped with all manner of winged contraptions, but failing to become airborne, crashed into the sea. Well documented and photographed in several editions. I also found an article on the ornithologist Sandy Johnson, told a reporter that his greatest wish was to attain flight like the birds he devoted his time and energy to. Alas you Dr Meecham fulfilled his wish, as good as killing him in the process."

"I'm a murderer now, am I? No better than Crippen, or that 'drowned in the bath' fella Smith! Well, I'll come clean. I did set up that competition and you aint to preach, both fellows knew what they were lettin' themselves in fer - they were excited as hell to be takin' part - a whole lot of planning went into it, a lot of care, safety a priority for them boys!"

Quivering with rage, Mr Holmes got up and smashed his stout ash stick down hard on the arm of the sofa, creating dust clouds in the room. The Padre managed to restrain him, but it was a close-run thing indeed.

"Safety! What those flimsy balsa wood and sailcloth deathtraps! Sandy was a marginal acquaintance of mine - you sent both men to certain doom and let me tell you - who was standing by to clean up the debris, the smashed wings, shoulder straps - leaving the scene clear so that the police should be distracted and the actual nature of this dangerous competition never become public knowledge - those men died for nothing. Alright, I admit they were foolhardy, but you dangled a large financial carrot."

Mr Exeter looked aghast, genuinely mortified and taken aback by Holme's outburst.

"They never, ever died in vain!" He shrieked, "How dare you infer such a thing Holmes! You have disappointed us - we thought you to be a man of reason, above average intelligence, if I told you that the lives of Mr's Lawson and Johnson were invaluable to scientific advancement - that during flight we were able to record on my instruments vital statistics relating to weightlessness and mental alertness, blood pressure, brain wave activity, so that Dr Meecham here, whose wealth is limitless, might accompany me to my true realm, the deep sea world, the vast submerged island of Atlantis! The first earth person from the surface of the modern world to achieve this - what then would you and the vicar say to that?"

"You from Atlantis, preposterous, next you'll be telling us you're firing some people carrying cannon balls into god's heaven through the clouds," laughed the Padre getting up to leave, assisting Mrs Simkins in the process.

"I think that is enough risible nonsense for one day, oh, and give my regards to my younger semblance, that scotch was quite first rate indeed."

"Holmes you old cuss, breathe one word of this and I'll alert my lawyers, turn your life into retirement hell, yer hear me!" Dr Meecham was yelling at the top of his voice. "Every dime you've got sucked away into legal fees and your time decimated away by endless New York and London office requests and court appearances."

A member of staff led Holmes and his friends through a side door and down some steps into the scenic gardens. They hurried around to fetch the motorcycle combo and the dog from out front of the manor.

Mrs Simkins as always proved her worth, for she had very advantageously slipped an important document into her shoulder purse when the butlers head was turned, having been (owing much to Dr Meecham's not inconsiderable vanity, and the strange Mr Exeter's compliance), given a tour of the rooms, the pair only too keen to show off the resplendent manor to an attractive member of the fairer sex.

(Paid for by Dr Meecham under Exeter's strange powerful influence)

A fortnight later, Dr Meecham and Exeter apparently hot footed to America to oversee a new industrial smelting plant – Pebblesea Manor was shuttered up, closed off to visitors. No word from New York lawyers received by Holmes thank heavens. He was pleased that a game of golf was on the cards at Seahaven links later that day with Dr Watson, who had returned from holiday.

Old Mr Holmes was taking his dog out along the cliffs after breakfast, able to mull things over, thinking clearly while walking.

Upon reflection, the plan, the diagram procured by Mrs Simkins he figured was plausible - yet in construction terms rather far-fetched. The police alas, saw the retired consultant's efforts, his findings as eccentric, far more concerned with following the old line of pursuing a mysterious cudgel bearing thug, credited as they saw it for the Pebblesea murders - disappointingly young Wilson had proved less than receptive.

Approaching Berwick Gap, the white painted coastguard's cottage in the foreground perched upon the edge under blue skies, the equally intense blue sea stretching further out to the horizon. The retired consulting detective was alerted by a bustle of activity.

Small figures ambling around on the shingle beach below.

Both man and dog hurried down the steep, twisty concrete steps, one hand firmly grasping the *warm-*

to-the-touch handrail. The sun was up, another fine summers day.

There was the toing and froing of police officers close to the surf, a rowing boat having been dragged ashore.

Onlookers, sea bathers were being encouraged to keep their distance.

An approaching individual whom Holmes rightly surmised to be an inspector of police had the impudence to regard him as part of the common herd.

"Move on, we want this area cleared sharpish. We can't 'ave just any old body stood about gawping - a police matter is currently in progress."

"I am not just any old body," Holmes replied curtly, doffing his straw boater, "I am Mr Sherlock

Holmes of Findon, and I incidentally play golf with your superior. Chief super of the county, Sir Cedric Evans."

"Beg pardon. Inspector Thorpe." The officer replied contritely. "Well sir, it looks like a boat capsized, two men drowned. Floating face down, craft in bits, must have struck the rocks in the small hours, tourist season an' all a crowd of sea bathers, but there we are."

At this juncture Holmes should have shown more restraint.

Understanding the tragic situation, let things be. Withdrawn to a more respectful distance further along the groynes - But alas, his curiosity got the better of him. Proved to be a greater pull and he latched onto the inspector like a clam.

The pair of bodies had been laid out on the beach after being recovered in a rowboat and were now concealed under tarpaulin. When the police drew back the sheets, Holmes caught a glimpse of both Dr Meecham and Mr Exeter. Blue lipped and waxy faced - that spoke to him not of a violent end, nor a struggle.

Inspector Thorpe directed that the drowned bodies should be dispatched on stretchers to the waiting van.

They proceeded at a sedate pace, with all dignity and respect, up the shingle beach, ready to negotiate the steep steps to attain at last the over path.

However, passing between a crowd gathered in flimsy sea bathing costumes, came the real shocker.

A peculiar hissing started up and Holmes was horrified to see, despite the corpses being only minutes earlier certified dead, life extinct - one of them started to breathe again, in a loud stertorous fashion.

Yet also remarkable, from beneath the blanket of this nearest stretcher, a scaly, webbed claw flopped limply down, the yellowish mottled talons twitching spasmodically, suddenly becoming still again.

Showing tact, the utmost perseverance in the line of duty, a number of stout-hearted constables, so as not to cause alarm amongst members of the public, swiftly conveyed the peculiar, altered body of Exeter into the rear of the police wagon. Whence doors slammed tightly shut before being firmly bolted.

Later that afternoon, talking with Dr Watson over lunch at the clubhouse, it was not hard to determine, armed with the plan, what incredible disaster had occurred. For at some stage, the deep-water vessel had broken up, maybe striking rocks out in the bay as the craft manoeuvred away from the beach area beneath the cliff. The shallows had proved more difficult than expected (maybe due to recent events at the manor house), far too soon Dr Meecham and Exeter had taken the decision to begin their journey down to Atlantis - forgetting any safety risk issues in their panic.

Another possibility - propulsion had failed. Either way, bits of wreckage and the bodies drifted on the current, surfacing further round the coast at Berwick Gap.

"My dear Holmes!" laughed Dr Watson, incredulous at the events. Having heard most of the whole episode, begun with the talk at Brambledean village hall. "At least, you shall not have to face those damned clever New York lawyers. Now that would have proved quite tiresome and that indeterminate fella Exeter even more so."

"I concur," concluded Holmes, raising his wine glass in solid agreement.

Epilogue

When next did old Mr Holmes walk his dog across the Downs to the lighthouse, he found it still to be draped in tarpaulin and scaffold. The forlorn structure a bit of an eyesore. So, it remained that way for many months until October came around. When high gale force winds blew the whole lot down and eventually out to sea.

Holmes observed that hardly any restoration had occurred, the only building work of note, a thick, impenetrable concrete floor laid at the base, thus any sign, even remote, that a sunken lift shaft had ever existed, was now smoothed over… obliterated.

The Sherlock Holmes Series

Sherlock By the Sea

Sherlock Holmes – The Wheelchair Mob

www.ingramcontent.com/pod-product-compliance
Lightning Source LLC
Chambersburg PA
CBHW030253100526
44590CB00012B/385